AF879034

TOO SMART

How to Take Charge of the Smart Tech in Your Life

TOM PYKE

Falls Grove Press
Arlington, VA

Copyright © 2020 Thomas N. Pyke, Jr. All rights reserved

First Printing 2020

All rights reserved. This book or any portion thereof may not be reproduced or used in any manner whatsoever without the express written permission of the publisher except for the use of brief quotations in a book review.

Falls Grove Press
Arlington, VA 22207
fallsgrovepress@gmail.com
www.tompyke.com

Editor and Project Manager: Marla Markman, www.MarlaMarkman.com
Cover and Interior Design: Andrew Chapman, SocialMotionPublishing.com
Copy Editor: Tammy Ditmore, eDitmore.com

Publisher's Cataloging-in-Publication Data
Names: Pyke, Tom, author.
Title: Too smart : how to take charge of the smart tech in your life / Tom Pyke.
Description: Includes index and bibliographical references. | Arlington, VA: Falls Grove Press, 2020.
Identifiers: LCCN 2019912941 | ISBN 978-1-7334665-0-9 (pbk.) | 978-1-7334665-1-6 (ebook)
Subjects: LCSH Human-computer interaction. | Consumers—Effect of technological innovations on. | Home automation. | Home computer networks. | Technological innovations—Social aspects. | Internet—Psychological aspects. | Internet—Social aspects. | Information technology—Moral and ethical aspects. | iPhone (Smartphone) | Mobile computing. | Application software. | BISAC COMPUTERS / General | COMPUTERS / Social Aspects / General | TECHNOLOGY & ENGINEERING / Social Aspects
Classification: LCC QA76.9.H85 .P95 2020 | DDC 004.019—dc23

ISBN: 978-1-7334665-0-9 (Print)
ISBN: 978-1-7334665-1-6 (eReaders)

Library of Congress Control Number: 2019912941

Printed in the United States of America

To All My Fellow Tech Lovers

CONTENTS

INTRODUCTION

Connecticut optometrists discovered a ransomware attack on their computers that encrypted all the data and disabled all the computers.[1] The attacker asked for a $4,000 ransom payment to restore the computers. The optometrists notified patients that their names, Social Security numbers, and some treatment information had been compromised. As a result, all the patients were potentially targets of identity theft.

A Tesla Model S car crashed into a stopped fire truck in San Jose, California.[2] This could happen when you are driving any car with adaptive cruise control, which enables your car to follow the vehicle in front of you as it speeds up and slows down. But sometimes this type of new safety technology gets confused when it encounters a stopped vehicle, and it may be too late for the driver to resume control unless they have been paying close attention.

Parents of a 2-year-old girl were startled when they heard a strange voice calling out to their daughter, Allyson, through a baby monitor in her room.[3] The voice from the baby monitor was not only calling their daughter by name, but using explicit language and telling Allyson to wake up. Anything connected to the internet can be compromised by ill-intended people if adequate precautions aren't taken to protect it.

A woman named Danielle in Portland, Oregon, who had

an Amazon Echo smart speaker, reported that someone received audio recordings of private conversations from Danielle's home.[4] Amazon investigators determined that the Echo woke up when it thought it heard the word "Alexa" and it started recording what was being said in the room. The Echo then thought it heard the words "to whom." It interpreted what was being said in the room as a name in the family contact list, after which it sent the audio recording by email to that person.

These are things that can and do happen. If you want to avoid—or survive—them in this age of new tech, this book is for you.

Who This Book Is For

This book is for people of any age and experience level, from hesitant first-time buyers to technology enthusiasts and early adopters. If you have high expectations for new technology and are dependent on it, you'll learn how to be a smart user of advanced technology that may have become "too smart."

If you plan to buy smartphones, ebook readers, PCs, and laptops, the tips in this book will help you make smart decisions. If you are interested in automating your home, you'll find tips to help you get started and to help you add more devices as you become comfortable with this kind of technology.

Maybe you're interested in joining the ranks of Alexa (who resides in the Amazon Echo and many other devices), Google Home, or other smart speaker owners. This book will help you sort through information about these new types of devices and more so you can decide whether you want one, and, if so, how to select the one that best meets your needs.

Are you interested in learning more about what's coming down the road, such as artificial intelligence that not only makes high-tech devices smarter, but could also make them partners in our daily lives? Perhaps you're ready to take a first step toward home automation and are looking for ideas about how to get started. This book can help you separate fact from fiction in the ads and reviews for new technology that is coming soon to our homes, our cars, and our workplaces. To give you a better overall picture as you make purchasing decisions, this book is intended to complement your use of tech review and shopping websites.

Each chapter will help you navigate the fast-changing, high-tech market. You'll find tips on how to deal with problems that are likely to occur, such as when your new gadget stops working or when it behaves unusually. Reasons for such behavior could include a problem with the device's software or a cyberattack or an intermittent connection to the internet.

We live in a brave new high-tech world, which can be confusing, frustrating—and exciting. If you follow the tips in this book, you will enjoy technology more and, as a result, enjoy life more.

A Little About the Author

I have spent over 40 years preparing to write this book so I can share what I have learned with you. I led research in advanced information technology (IT) for over 20 years, creating innovative new computer systems and networks and developing guidance on computer security. I designed innovative computer hardware and wrote new software that made computers more responsive to users. I led projects that predicted technology trends, giving me a good background to guide you toward the future of high-tech devices. I have led the evaluation and application of IT as the chief information officer, or IT leader, of large organizations.

As an early adopter, I know firsthand the difficulties of pushing the envelope of the latest technology when it wasn't quite ready for prime time. This combination of research leadership, technology forecasting, and managing the application of advanced IT makes me well-qualified to help you thrive on new technology and survive the pitfalls that you will face along the way.

New high-tech devices come on the market all the time, so you may find some of the references to technology a little dated. That's inevitable in a book like this, but I have invested a lot of effort to make most of the book somewhat timeless.

How This Book Is Organized

Here's how to get the most out of all the information in this book. If you read through the chapters in order, you'll get the complete story of new technology and how to benefit from it. But you could also scan through it, focusing on topics that are interesting to you. For example, if you're curious about how to protect yourself and your high-tech devices from cyberattacks, go directly to Chapter 4, "Watch Out for Cybersecurity." If you are intrigued by why our new technology has become so complex, you may want to spend extra time on Chapters 6, 7, and 8. To develop your plan of attack, here is a short summary of each chapter.

Chapter 1: Surrounded by New Technology

We are surrounded by technology wherever we are. It's our constant companion at home, at the office, when we drive or take public transportation, and even when we walk on the street. Technology is pervasive in our lives, and we tend to take it for granted. Technology can make our lives easier, more productive, and fun.

Chapter 2: New Technology Euphoria

We often think "newer" is synonymous with progress. We don't usually go into a store saying "show me some new technology."

But we sure come close to it. Planning your purchase of new, high-tech things can result in a better match to your needs. Taking the time to evaluate alternatives can temper the natural excitement that most of us have as we prepare to bring home new smartphones, PCs, home automation devices, and other high-tech gizmos.

Chapter 3: Downsides of New Technology

These new high-tech devices can seem confusing and hard to use, partly because they have so many features. Sometimes we start relating more to technology than to people, and we have to ask who is in charge—us or the new gadget. Some of these new things have the potential to invade our privacy, watching us and listening to us.

Chapter 4: Watch Out for Cybersecurity

One downside of our new technology is so worrisome that it deserves its own chapter. Cybersecurity attacks are happening so often that it's hard to keep track of them, and we are vulnerable to these attacks because we have become so dependent on our new technology. This chapter contains over 30 tips to help you to avoid being the victim of a cyberattack.

Chapter 5: Technology—A Historical Perspective

It's easier to understand new technology if you know something about its history. In this chapter, you'll learn how technology came of age and became such an important part of our lives. Scientists and engineers built highly innovative new systems and networks that have made technology incredibly useful to us, but at the same time, these well-intended people introduced so much complexity that high-tech devices sometimes don't work as expected and can be threatened by cyberattacks.

Chapter 6: Everything Is So Complex

The technology we depend on every day has become complex, which is the result of the large number of features in our high-tech devices and the software necessary to implement them. This complexity leads to fragility, where devices can fail for no obvious reason. It can lead to vulnerabilities in our devices, which make them more susceptible to cyberattacks. Also, buying devices with functionality we don't need can lead to unnecessary complexity.

Chapter 7: Let's Reboot

Complexity in our high-tech devices creates uncertainty. Often, a programmable device doesn't know what to do next. The system can get hung up because of software errors or because it faces input it doesn't recognize or other conditions it has never seen before. The solution is often to reboot.

Chapter 8: The Things Are Coming!

The Internet of Things is the concept of making physical things around us smart, then connecting them to each other and to "the cloud." Automated home thermostats, smart speakers, and systems that turn lights on and off and automatically lock doors are part of the Internet of Things. These types of devices introduce additional complexity and risk into our lives, and they are especially vulnerable to cyberattacks.

Chapter 9: How to Survive New Technology

We are surrounded by new technology. All day we are subjected to a barrage of information from our complex smartphones, smart speakers, smart cars, and more. Yet we can't live without this technology. So, how can we take full advantage of this tech without losing our grip? The tips in this chapter help us simplify, tune out, and manage our smart tech before it manages us. While we are developing "friendships" with our high-tech helpers, like Siri and Alexa, we have to be careful not to lose touch with our human friends.

Chapter 10: What's in Our Future?

The march of new technology continues at what seems to be an ever-increasing pace. The technology will be smarter and smarter, maybe even as smart as we are. Technology will assist us as we drive our cars, and by 2030, we are likely to have true self-driving cars. While we are likely to be partners with our technology as we depend on it throughout our day, we also want to remain "in charge." A number of knowledgeable people are concerned that artificial intelligence (AI) could eventually spell doom for humankind, but that is not likely, especially if we are successful in using human-machine collaboration to outperform machines working by themselves. But we may occasionally feel overwhelmed by tech and need to take a technology time-out from time to time.

Chapter 11: Continuing to Love Our New Technology

We want our technology to be smart, but not too smart. Technological developments will play an increasingly important role in making our lives better. We will continue to love our new technology, yet we will become even more dependent on it and will grow more accustomed to rebooting or working around the problems it introduces, without realizing we are adapting to our high-tech devices. We'll want to take advantage of all the benefits technology provides us, while taking precautions to protect ourselves from cyberattacks and other threats. We will love our technology more if we are knowledgeable about it and its limitations and realize what it will be able to do for us in the future.

Throughout the book, you'll find:

- "Key Words" that define terms that are used in the book.
- "Smart Tips" that are recommendations to help you make informed choices regarding high-tech products and services and to help you avoid cyberattacks and other problems.
- "For the Tech Curious" boxes that offer deeper insight into the technology.

You'll also find a list of key points at the end of each chapter to help you focus on the most important takeaways.

Now that you know what you can look forward to, turn the page and let's get started!

CHAPTER 1

SURROUNDED BY NEW TECHNOLOGY

WE ARE SURROUNDED by technology. At home and at work, in our cars, and as we walk down the street with our cell phones in hand and our earbuds blaring our favorite music, we immerse ourselves in our personal tech world. We love what technology does for us, and we have become dependent on it for much of our way of life. But depending on high-tech devices introduces some challenges that we have to recognize and put into perspective. Among these challenges is that technology may be becoming "too smart." Are new smartphones and smart speakers always doing what we want them to do, or are they sometimes taking on a life of their own, perhaps spying on us? We want to enjoy and depend on high-tech devices, but we want to know that we are still in charge and that technology hasn't taken over!

We Are More Aware of Technology Around Us

We are now more acutely aware of technology, especially new digital technology, because it stares us in the face every time we pick up our smartphone, open our laptop, or connect to the internet. Is my iPhone beeping again? Is it an email or a text? Maybe it's a notification or an alert about the weather or a local community emergency. Maybe it's something new that a friend has posted on Facebook or an alert about a lower gas price near me.

We see the face of technology in the things around us. When we think of technology, we think mostly of things that go beep and bonk, things that are digital. We don't necessarily think of the technology behind our clothes, shoes, tennis rackets, golf clubs, or modern medicine. That technology is not as "in your face" as the new digital technology that is more obvious and intrusive.

Historically, technology has not been as obvious in our lives, although there has been a lot of it all around us for many years. It was behind the scenes, making our appliances, TVs, cars, and other things work. Even a decade or so ago we didn't face technology every second of every day—or at least it didn't seem that way. Technology has been an important part of everyone's lives for many years, beginning with early stone tools 3 million years ago, up to the invention of the wheel and clocks, the printing press, and computers. (Be sure to read Chapter 5, "Technology—A Historical Perspective," for more about the history of technology.)

When we are flooded by new things all the time, it seems like the speed of technological advances is faster. Maybe technological advances didn't come as often in the past as they have in recent years, or maybe we are just more sensitive to technology in our lives than people were in the past.

We live in an advertising-driven world, one in which ads about new technological things are "pushed" at us on TV, in newspapers and magazines, and on the internet. Ads are pushed at us when we are searching for something using Google and when we are viewing the news or looking at Facebook. Many of the "free" online services we depend on every day rely on advertising revenue for their existence. Our views about new high-tech devices—when we decide to buy them and use them—are influenced by these ads.

Smart Tip

When you feel you are being pushed too hard by technology around you, try turning off some of your notifications and putting your smartphone aside for a while. You have control over your high-tech devices, though sometimes it may not feel that way.

Our Fast-Paced Lives Call for Fast Technology

Our fast-paced lives can lead to increasing demands on the technology that surrounds us, requiring a quicker response from high-tech devices. We want to go at our own pace and not be hindered by slower, older technology. Our new technology must support our fast-paced lifestyle. We depend on speedy communication at home and work, and when we are mobile. We use "fast tools" like tweeting and texting, using short snippets and abbreviations instead of full sentences.

Our lives sometimes seem faster because we are very busy, and we need help creating more hours in the day. We can do this with technology that helps us be more productive at home and at work. We can do more in less time and with less effort. We can also increase our productivity by using technology-enabled services, such as for pickup and delivery of food and packages and for on-demand transportation through companies like Uber. When we are driving a car, we can save time by relying on GPS-based navigation to direct us to the fastest route and deliver traffic information, whether "over the air" by satellite or local radio to our car navigation system or through the internet to our phone's mapping and navigation app.

We want it all, and we want it now. We are spoiled by

streaming video like Netflix, instant search results from Google and instant access to any website. We live in an impatient world and have developed high expectations that our technology will respond quickly when we make a request. We are annoyed when we must wait while our PC starts up. We are impatient when it takes "too long" for everything to boot up in our new cars before we can use navigation and infotainment systems.

We are usually tolerant of response-time delays if the wait seems reasonable, given what is being done for us. However, it can still be frustrating when we can't touch our keyboard while waiting for a web transaction to complete for fear of being double charged or having something else horrible happen to us.

In today's fast-paced world we frequently drive ourselves to multitask. We expect smartphones, PCs, and the internet to multitask as well, or at least be so quick that they appear to be doing so. Our expectations are greater with every new smartphone model or other high-tech thing.

We Want New Features

New technology often brings us new features or capabilities, such as TVs that support video streaming through the internet, smart speakers, and cars that warn us when another car is in our blind spot. Technology makes possible new features that soon become essential in our lives. The automated emergency braking system in my car detects a car slowing down too fast in front of me. First, it flashes a red warning signal, then it taps the brakes, and then, if necessary, it applies the brakes with full force. This capability is now slated to become standard in almost all new cars sold in the US by 2022.[5]

New technology that we are dependent on now uses capabilities that make devices easier to use and better matched to our current ways of doing things. For example,

Key Word

A **smart speaker**, such as the Amazon Echo, which is home to "Alexa," listens for an awake word, like "Alexa," so we can tell it what to do. It responds by playing music or taking other actions like turning on the lights or sending messages.

smartphones incorporate several functions that we had in older cell phones, in addition to many new functions, in one integrated package. Smartphones have become mobile personal computers that offer lots of computational capability and storage, as well as a web browser, "apps," and high-speed connectivity to the internet.

Many people have become dependent on wearable fitness bands and health-related smartphone apps, some of which are connected to fitness bands. New health-care technology has appeared in doctors' offices and hospitals, with high-tech digital imagers, body function monitors, electronic record-keeping systems that flag unusual information for doctors to review, and other high-tech equipment, such as the da Vinci robotic surgical arm and radiation treatment systems that focus the radiation where it is needed.

In our homes, many of us use new technology for home automation, to control lighting, heating and air conditioning; electronic locks and other security functions; and entertainment systems. Smartphones can be used to control many home automation devices. This type of technology application, that allows things around us to connect to other things and to the internet, is generally referred to as the Internet of Things. Check out Chapter 8, "The Things Are Coming!"

It Makes Us Happier

All the new, high-tech gizmos around us contribute to our happiness, enabling us to have more fun and to enjoy life. We watch TV with content delivered via cable and through internet-streaming video. We play video games, and we search the web with Google and other tools.

We expect these harbingers of happiness to incorporate the latest technology. Our new TV has to be high definition (HD), maybe even ultra HD! We make dinner reservations online and expect the restaurants to give us just as good a table when we reserve online as when we call them. We use wearable fitness bands to help keep us healthy, monitoring our bodies as we exercise and even when we sleep.

Technology has become essential to our way of life. We are connected to other people in ways we never imagined using social networking apps and websites. Technology extends our reach, both around us and to distant parts of the world. We feel happy when we touch a button on our smartphone to check email or to view a text. It makes us happy when we get the latest news or the gossip from friends on Facebook. It makes us happy when we discover something new and interesting by searching the web. It makes us feel good to know that the world is responding to our needs, second by second.

Many of the things that make us happier using new technology involve computers. These "embedded" computers are often inside our TVs and smart appliances. We don't see the embedded computers or processors, and we don't interface directly with them. They are usually tightly integrated into the fabric of the high-tech things that we depend on every day, and they give these things added functionality at a potentially lower cost.

Rushing to buy new high-tech gizmos may, however, provide only temporary happiness. Buying something new and exciting may make us feel good for a while, but the principle

What Do You Expect?

Satisfaction with technology in our lives is determined, in part, by our expectations. Robb Rutledge, a cognitive and computational neuroscientist at University College London, has reported the results of his studies that show happiness depends not on how well things are going, but whether they are going better than expected.[213] He introduced the concept of "momentary well-being," which is based on the degree to which we are surprised when something pleasant happens. We often live in the moment, without focusing on the past or the future. You could say that with new technology in our lives we are "living in the second," not just the moment. Things happen fast, and they are tied to what we are doing at the time. They are also tied to the technology we are using at the moment and to the people with whom we are currently connected in our lives, at home, at work, and at play.

that psychologists refer to as "hedonic adaption" is likely to kick in, and we may take the new gizmo for granted after a while. In other words, the happiness of having the new gizmo may fade over time.[6]

We Are Comfortable with Our New Technology

We have become so comfortable with new technology that people say we sometimes relate better to our PCs and our smartphones than we do to each other. We now have a high level of comfort using email and texting, Facebook and Twitter. In fact, we are so comfortable communicating this way that we blurt out things on the internet that we wouldn't dare say in person.

Some of these "instant" emails, texts, or tweets can get

us in real trouble. Sometimes we wish we hadn't hit the send button. Fortunately, Gmail now has a feature to help in this situation; you can "undo" a sent message within 30 seconds after it was sent.

Is it the impersonality of the technology that causes us to let our guard down? Do we think things are more "anonymous" on the internet, even though our name or online ID is attached to things we post? Or maybe it's because texting and email doesn't feel as real as person-to-person communication. Maybe we adopt a different persona when we interact using technology than we do with old fashioned personal conversation.

Once we have new technology and are comfortable with it, we are reluctant to give it up. A 2018 Pew Research Center survey concludes that 50 percent of surveyed adults would find it very hard or impossible to give up their internet access, and 52 percent of them wouldn't give up their cell phone.[7] We have become dependent on technology—and we like it that way.

New Technology Seems Like Progress

New technology in the things around us and innovation in general is often equated with progress. But progress is not always definable, and it is not always a path to a better future. The importance of progress has become central to our thinking process, and the term is often overused. It has been said that progress is an increase in well-being, or quality of life.[8] Progress, in the minds of many of us, equates to new technology, with new models of TVs and smartphones and faster internet connections. Back in the old days, Ronald Reagan was featured in GE commercials saying "Progress is our most important product!"

Sometimes new appliances, cars, and other things don't have quite the same appeal, especially if we remember the older things "fondly," like a washing machine with the mechanical knob that you turn to set the cycle and timing before hitting the "on" button. Newer, high-tech devices are sometimes harder to use and may require fiddling with more controls and displays to make them work well. Also, some new features added to appliances and cars and other things can be inducements to buy them rather than genuine advances that improve our long-term customer experience. Do we really need 25 cycles on our washers? Can't 10 cycles do everything we need? Do we need an 8-cylinder engine with a turbo charger in our car, or even a 6-cylinder engine? Fuel-saving 4-cylinder engines can now accelerate just as fast as older 8-cylinder engines, and they feel almost as smooth.

Progress with new high-tech gadgets may be making people lazier. Everyone expects technology to make their lives easier and to reduce the amount of work people have to do. Well, this does happen to some extent. But new technology can sometimes lead to unforeseen problems. Pilots may spend so much time on autopilot that they sometimes neglect their oversight role and may even be in danger of losing valuable flying skills because they don't get enough experience flying the plane. The engineer or operator of a subway train may depend so much on automatic operation that they become too relaxed in oversight of the train's operation and unable to respond well in an emergency.

Similarly, driving a car is becoming more and more automated, with adaptive cruise control and lane departure warning and other features, so humans are doing less and less "overseeing" of their cars' operation. What happens when the human's attention is urgently needed and the driver is distracted with texting, or maybe even snoozing?

The Power to Transform

New technology results from innovation, which is then

implemented in things we use, the things that surround us. The Wharton School of the University of Pennsylvania has developed a list of the most important innovations over the last 30 years—inventions that have transformed the world.[9] At the top of the list are the internet, broadband communications, and the World Wide Web. Then come PCs and laptops, mobile phones, and email. DNA testing and sequencing and magnetic resonance imaging (MRI) are also on the list, along with microprocessors, fiber optics, light emitting diodes (LEDs), liquid crystal displays (LCDs), GPS systems, bar code scanners, and ATMs.

Our appetite is whetted when we are exposed to new high-tech things, and we sometimes have little patience with the "old." We must have gadgets based on new technology that provide improved performance and functionality. Our expectations go higher with every new technological advance based on the latest innovations, and we are reluctant to give up technology once we have incorporated it into our daily lives. But which of our new high-tech gizmos do we really need?

Do we need a smart TV that listens to us and watches as we gesture to it? Or is a TV like that "too smart"? Maybe we don't want our TV to be listening to us or watching us. Some smart TVs report what we are watching to companies that send us ads based on what we watch. We may not want to be spied on by our TV, but if we want a TV with a high-quality picture we may have to accept these other "smart" features as part of the package because this is becoming the only way we can buy a TV. We can always try to disable the microphone, camera, and other features that we don't want in our lives. The camera on my smart TV is turned off in the settings, and I have also put black electrical tape over it so it can't watch us.

Older technology is still in our lives, too. But sometimes older technology fades away because it is no longer viable to make products using it. By using newer technology, the cost of feature-laden TVs and other high-tech gadgets has been going down dramatically.

Any new technology evolves over time. Historian Thomas Hughes calls this "technological momentum."[10] A new technology is malleable at an early stage and can be shaped by designers as well as those who use the technology. But once the technology has become widely implemented, change becomes much more difficult. You could say that the technology develops "a mind of its own"! There has even been a school of thought that technology drives the development of the society's social structure and cultural values, a concept said to have been introduced by American sociologist and economist Thorstein Veblen.[11]

We are used to our TVs, cars, and other things having high-tech functionality far beyond the devices available just a few years ago. Smart TVs have web browsers and apps, just like we are accustomed to on our PCs and smartphones. But the user interface for these types of functions on our PCs and smartphones has become highly refined and easy to use. TV manufacturers are having a hard time providing a user interface for these functions that meets our expectations for ease of use. This is especially so as TV manufacturers now have to compete with Apple TV, Amazon Fire TV, Roku, and other easy-to-use devices that provide capabilities like easy search and video selection, as well as fast video streaming of movies and other content along with convenient fast forward, pause, and other functions.

Likewise, some cars include web functionality in their infotainment systems, but it has generally been awkward to use and has limited functionality. To correct this problem, car manufacturers have joined forces with Apple and Google to use familiar smartphone interfaces and technology in cars, called Apple Car Play and Android Auto.

However, as we introduce new capabilities dependent on new technology, we generally also introduce greater complexity, which can make devices more likely to fail or to do unusual things. Consider how we sometimes have to reboot things be-

Life Is Better with New Technology

New technology makes the things around us work better and makes them easier to use. Think about how unreliable our cars were 30 years ago—the engines, the tires, all the parts that failed often or wore out quickly. We take for granted that we only have to push a button to raise and lower the windows, rather than turning a crank handle. The windshield wipers work all the time rather than slowing down and speeding up and sometimes stopping. Our headlights are bright and properly aimed. Steering and braking are smoother and more reliable, and new suspensions contribute to better control and a better ride. Our cars are also more comfortable inside, with easily controlled heating and air conditioning, and they aren't prone to overheating when driving up a steep grade in hot weather.

cause they have stopped working properly. Rebooting means to restart something, by unplugging it and then plugging it in or by pressing a reset button. Maybe new technology isn't all roses, after all. Stay tuned for a discussion of the "thorns among the roses" in Chapter 3, "Downsides of New Technology," and Chapter 4, "Watch Out for Cybersecurity."

We Love Technology . . . Most of the Time

Most of the time technology does what we now expect, and it

works just fine. But sometimes technology doesn't work as advertised, and it fails in unusual ways, just when we have become dependent on it. Sometimes we are in the middle of purchasing something online and everything freezes. You're left wondering if the problem is with your PC or smartphone. Is it your internet connection that has stopped working? Has the website gone down or become overloaded? It's often hard to tell.

When our high-tech devices fail too frequently, we realize that new technology is somewhat fragile. Why does our new technology seem so powerful, yet sometimes seem to be so fragile? It's because of the complexity of new technology. Why have we become so dependent on such a fragile technological infrastructure? We have no choice if we want the benefits of new technology, but there are steps we can take to help improve the way technology works for us. You'll find these steps in the Smart Tips boxes throughout the book. Read about complexity

Key Word

The **web**, short for the World Wide Web, is an application that runs on the internet and gives us access to pictures, videos, and text and enables us to engage in transactions, such as buying things. A **website** is software running on a server computer out on the internet, such as Amazon.com. A **web browser** is software on a PC or a smartphone that connects a user to a website and displays text, pictures, and other content from that website.

and fragility in Chapter 2, "New Technology Euphoria," and in Chapter 6, "Everything Is So Complex."

In this chapter, we focused on the forces that have increased our dependency on new technology. When technology is constantly in our face and we frequently see ads for new high-tech gizmos, this sets the stage for our dependency on it. Our need to support our faster-paced lives with new technology drives us to seek devices with new and "better" features. New technology also introduces challenges, such as high-tech devices that fail sometimes, but we have learned that it is worth the effort to deal with these nuisances. In later chapters, we will further explore the challenges and downsides of adopting new high-tech devices.

Smart Tip

The first thing to try when things aren't working as expected when connected to a website is to wait a few minutes and try again. It often helps to close the web browser and open it again, then try to connect to the same website.

After this discussion of the new technology that surrounds us and how it can be great as well as frustrating, the next chapter offers some thoughts about the euphoria we sometimes feel when we go to a store to buy high-tech gizmos or when we impulsively buy something online that "we can't do without"—with just the press of a button. We may be euphoric when we think about new things, but our long-term interests can usually be best met if we think before we buy, perhaps getting some advice first.

Key Points

- We are now more acutely aware of the technology around us. It's not in the background anymore. It's in our face!
- Technology may be becoming too smart. We want to benefit from it, but we want to be in charge.
- Our technology needs to move at our fast pace to be most helpful to us.
- We love our high-tech devices when they do what we expect and when they work just fine. But it can be frustrating when they hang up or do other unexpected things.
- New technology brings us new capabilities that we find incredibly useful, and, as a result, we have become increasingly dependent on high-tech in our lives. Our high-tech devices make us happier, and we would be reluctant to give them up. We have become comfortable with our new technology.
- We are part of the march of progress around us, driven by technological innovation. New technology makes the things around us work better and makes them easier to use.
- We have learned that it is worth the effort to deal with the challenges that new technology sometimes introduces.

CHAPTER 2

NEW TECHNOLOGY EUPHORIA

WE OFTEN THINK that newer is better. It's like the adage "the grass is always greener on the other side of the fence." Nowhere is that statement truer than in buying and using new technology.

In the US, new technology is considered flashy and seductive, with hordes ready to jump on the new technology bandwagon and be early adopters. The only justification needed is that it's cool, new, and different.

You could say we have "technology euphoria." We don't usually go into a store saying "show me some new technology," but we don't go into a store asking for a good deal on older model PCs or laptops, either. We want the latest model with all the bells and whistles. The same goes for our smartphones. We usually want the latest model because we believe the new capabilities will provide useful benefits, which we deem worthy of the extra money. However, the price of smartphones has risen so sharply, and the perceived benefits are sometimes so marginal, that some people are now asking for older, less expensive models that still have relatively new technology and capabilities.

This chapter is intended to rein in that euphoria a tad so you don't get carried away buying things on the other side of the fence that you don't need. Maybe some of our "needs" are

Key Word

A **smartphone** is a mobile phone (a cell phone) that functions not only as a phone, but also as a powerful computer that connects you to the internet. A smartphone supports lots of "apps," which are downloaded applications, such as for Facebook, Twitter, and CNN. In this book, the term "smartphone" is used to refer to all brands and types of smartphones, including those that use the Apple iOS operating system and those that use variants of the Android operating system, including smartphones from Samsung.

created by ads that bombard us or by our friends who have new gizmos, leading us to want one, too. It can pay to look carefully and think a bit before purchasing high-tech devices, rather than just buying what you feel like buying. Well, maybe you can get carried away just a little, but, overall, you will be better off if you stand back and breathe before you jump in, feet first, to buy every new thing in sight.

This chapter helps you think about which new high-tech devices you really need and the external pressures you may face, like ads pushing new products or peers who offer friendly recommendations. It introduces the concept of using logic along with emotions in your high-tech selection process and recommends being cautious about the newest, bleeding-edge things that might not be ready for prime time. It then guides you through identifying and selecting from among alternative new devices and buying them online or in a store.

Why Do I Buy Things?

As we seek new technology, we are responding to our perceived need for something "bright and shiny" that will be fun and useful—and all wrapped up at a reasonable price. At the same time, we are responding to needs that reflect the world we live in and are probably influenced by what our friends and colleagues have, and how they go on and on about the great new high-tech gizmo they have bought. Being bombarded with ads for new, high-tech products also gets our attention, but there is something more to our interest in new technology and our drive to have the latest and greatest. We have become enamored by new technology, and we want more and more. Yes, you could have a touch of tech euphoria!

When we prepare to buy something, we develop, either explicitly or implicitly, a list of needs or requirements, which may be framed in terms of functionality or features, perhaps coupled with needed performance, such as computing speed or camera resolution.

One way to look at the needs technology helps meet is to examine Maslow's hierarchy of needs. Maslow defined basic physiological requirements and safety as minimum needs. Self-actualization and self-esteem are at the top of the list.[12] For example, technology can help us meet some of our safety needs, by enabling us to call for emergency assistance, and our need for love and belonging, by keeping us in touch with family and friends. Technology even helps us achieve greater self-esteem when other people respect us or think highly of us partly because we have the latest technology. For some people, access to technology helps them be more creative and to thrive in their lives. New technology appears to have the greatest impact when it can help us fulfill the highest level of need, self-actualization, which is the need to be good, to be fully alive, and to find meaning in life.

Conceptually, one reason many of us buy new things is that we are "aspirational people."[13] We aspire to be better, to have better things, and we feel better when we buy and use new things. While recognizing that we have these kinds of needs and aspirations, it is helpful to try to differentiate things that are nice to have from those you must have.

It is quite possible that we couldn't go back to old technology even if we wanted to continue using older things. The older devices may not be made anymore, and they may no longer be supported by technical help and software updates. It is likely the older devices cost more to make than new ones, and there is a limited market for the older ones. Even today's lower-end smartphone models use a lot of advanced technology.

They Made Me Do It

We didn't necessarily ask for all these products and services that incorporate new technology; many were developed and marketed by companies that are trying to induce us to buy new things in order to enhance their bottom line. We are bombarded by ads and news stories about new, high-tech things all the time. Although we may be able to get a better deal on a lower performance device or an older model, we are influenced by ads that tout the advantages of the latest models, such as higher-resolution displays, better connectivity, and ease of use. No wonder we are constantly seeking that other side of the fence and find it difficult to determine what we realistically need.

Companies designing new products and services are raising our expectations. But, perhaps, we are also in a world in which the name of the game for technology manufacturers is to design and sell new things that become "obsolete as rapidly as possible so that the next iteration of smartphones, PCs, or cars can be sold to a willing market."[14] New devices usually do have significantly new capabilities. But they sometimes seem to be designed to wear out or become obsolete in a relatively short time. We have seen this process work for decades with new cars, PCs, and other things.

Sometimes it's the software that's the problem. Newer versions of software operating systems generally need more memory and a faster processor. Devices wear out, too, with heavy usage over time, especially for things like physical switches, displays, and batteries. Are we being pressured, in effect, to buy new technology by the companies that offer it or risk losing capabilities we have become accustomed to?

Less Emotion, More Logic

We are excited about the new things we are about to buy, and we often get even more excited after we buy them. It's fun to shop for new technology and to bring home a brand-new high-tech gizmo. We often don't comparison shop like we do for some low-tech things like clothes or furniture. We just go online, take a quick look, then buy the latest version of our favorite older thing. Sometimes, we get upset when we find out that our favorite thing is no longer manufactured. We often have a personal investment in a device we have learned to use, that works well, and that we are comfortable with. So, it is a personal loss when it no longer works and we can't replace it.

Some new high-tech products are especially exciting. Voice input using Siri and Alexa is fun to use. We even talk to our car to help control navigation and other functions. Using gestures to control the TV and the car has potential but seems to be mostly a gimmick. In these examples, users are actively involved by touching, talking, or moving their hands and arms around. This personal involvement helps us develop an emotional attachment to high-tech gadgets. Once our emotions are

Smart Tip

Try to keep your emotions in check as you consider buying new high-tech devices. Watch out for "hyper-euphoria"!

involved, it becomes harder to use logic and facts to make decisions about technology purchases.

That's important to know because logic is what should be primarily driving your purchase decision. Before you buy any gadget, you should look closely at the description, then decide how it stacks up against your needs. If you can do a hands-on test of a demonstration version, do so, and not just casually. Give it a real workout doing the kinds of things you would do if you owned it. For some types of things, like smartphones, new high-end devices with all the bells and whistles can be so expensive that we may have to choose among smartphones that are "less exciting" but will still meet our highest-priority needs.

You have your own, real needs and those apparent needs inspired by ads and maybe tricky things developers and marketers do to steer us to new products. You have factored in the emotions that may be in play going into the purchase. Now

Smart Tip

Evaluate a new product you are considering against your personal needs. Test it through hands-on use if possible.

it's time to develop a game plan for buying your new high-tech device so you will have a better chance of getting one that meets your needs.

Plan Your Purchase

Planning a purchase may seem obvious to you or like an unnecessary complication. But planning your purchase can help you think about how and why you choose new high-tech gadgets before you buy them so they work better for you after you own them.

As a first step in this process, you should identify and characterize what you are interested in buying. What is the general type of high-tech device you are interested in (for example, a 55-inch TV or a video doorbell)? Take a preliminary look at what is available that may meet your needs. At this point, it will help you narrow the options, because it can be quite confusing if you walk into a store and must pick from among 5 or 10 different things that you may want to consider.

Many of us are predisposed to playing it by ear when we shop online or walk into a store. Sometimes we even buy more than we need. If we can't use a feature today, it will be there when we may need it tomorrow. This doesn't mean you have to know exactly what you want to buy before you start looking or even when you are about to make the purchase. But thinking about it ahead of time will help you enjoy your purchase more afterward. Don't worry, following this process doesn't rule out the occasional, just-for-fun, impulse buy.

So What Am I Going to Buy?

Suppose you want a new smartphone, smart speaker, Wi-Fi router, or some other tech device. First, develop a clear picture of what you want to buy. Identify the capabilities or features you need most, such as a smartphone that works well everywhere, without dropping calls where you usually make calls. Try to say no to features you may never need and say no to performance far beyond anything you could likely use.

It is often hard to decide if we need certain features, such as a higher refresh rate on a TV, which may mean less flicker, or an LED light bulb that can change colors. So, try to obtain enough information about features and performance to determine what really matters. Scouring buying guides and specifications may still not be enough for this analysis, and we don't have all day to perform an in-depth review for everything we are thinking about buying. You must set a balance you are comfortable with, between reviewing everything to death and buying without doing any homework.

Smart Tip

Try not to get confused by features and performance that may not matter to you.

Try to put a new product in perspective relative to similar products you have used in the past. How much better is this one than the older ones? Does it work significantly better? Does it look better? Is it significantly faster? Or is it just version 2.2 of the same kind of thing, and you are feeling sad because you only have version 2.1?

You don't have to make a career out of this kind of evaluation. You just need to take a few steps to be sure you are making a good decision. When I get all excited about a new

Key Words

Wi-Fi is a wireless local network that enables smartphones, PCs, and other devices to communicate with each other and the internet. The **internet** is a worldwide network that interconnects computers, smartphones, and other devices. A **Wi-Fi router**, sometimes called a gateway, is a device that connects your home to the internet through your internet service provider, through a cable TV connection or in some other way. The router also has a **Wi-Fi "radio"** that enables our smartphones and other things to connect wirelessly to the internet through the router. A Wi-Fi radio consists of one or more radio frequency transmitters and receivers and one or more antennas. It's not an old fashioned AM or FM radio! Our smartphones, smart tablets, PCs, and smart home devices, such as smart thermostats, have Wi-Fi radios that connect them to Wi-Fi routers and other Wi-Fi devices. You can also have hardwired connections to the router using an Ethernet cable.

product, I have found it helpful to wait a few weeks or a month after it has been announced, then check reviews online after the product has been delivered. If the product is available on a shopping site such as Amazon, check reviews from people who say they have purchased it.

Be sure not to rely solely on a salesperson or the ads for a new product. If you had devised a new product and were selling it, would you tell potential buyers about the deficiencies of the product compared to similar products? To make them sound more believable, some salespeople throw in a few little gems about the product's shortcomings as part of their sales spiel. But you must do the work, studying available information about the competing products you are considering before deciding which one to buy. In general, the more informed you are, the better your decision will be. Do enough shopping around and ask enough questions to make yourself comfortable with your purchase.

Then, think about how much you really need to buy this new product. It if means a lot to you, and you have, in your mind, decided to buy something, then go right ahead. If it isn't quite that important to you, then consider giving the decision time to simmer before you take the plunge. As part of this process, think hard about whether this is the right time to move ahead.

It's OK to Have Preferences

Sometimes we prefer to buy something that is similar to a device we have used in the past, rather than one that is different, even if that one seems better. This preference is a human tendency sometimes referred to as "cognitive fluency."[15] This tendency also explains why you may stay with a brand or service provider you have used before, and it even helps explain why you often order the same things from the menu at your favorite restaurant. I sometimes take this "easy out," especially when I have been satisfied in the past by a brand and don't want to spend a lot of time and energy researching alternatives.

You may have different preferences than other people as you search for just the right technology to meet your needs for desktop or laptop computing. Many people like a PC that works something like the original IBM PC. This basic architecture has been perpetuated by a wide range of manufacturers over the years. It still relies on Microsoft software, the Windows operating system and the Office productivity suite, including Word and Excel. Laptop PCs have gained a lot of ground on desktop PCs, but the old IBM PC architecture is widely available in both desktops and laptops. It is the favorite of many of us and continues to be the mainstay for personal computing in most businesses. However, along the way, the world of Apple

For the Tech Curious

As people seek new technology, they are generally looking for more capability and features than they have, which leads to more complex technology than in the past. Generally, new devices have more hardware components and many more lines of software code. The addition of features to a device adds complexity and tends to make it more fragile because more things can go wrong. In addition, the device's software was likely programmed by a team of people, sometimes so large that no one person knows how all the software works.

In fact, modern high-tech devices are so complex that it is impossible to test them fully before releasing them to consumers. So, consumers become part of the testing process, guinea pigs for the latest devices. Based on what is learned "under fire" in the hands of consumers, manufacturers issue "new releases" of software, called "updates" or "patches," that add new features and fix problems that have been identified and, hopefully, don't create new ones. Read Chapter 6, "Everything Is So Complex," for a discussion of technological complexity and how it affects you.

Macintosh has taken a firm hold, with Apple Mac devotees fervently believing their technology is the best. MacBooks and iMacs are very popular and capable. In this book, the word "PC" is used to refer to both PCs with the old IBM PC architecture and to Apple Macs.

We have also developed preferences for smartphones and smart tablets. By the numbers, smartphones from several manufacturers that run the Google Android operating system are in the majority. But Apple iPhone users usually believe strongly that their smartphones are the best. It's fine to have a favorite type of smartphone or car or anything else, and to give greater consideration to your favorite as you make buying decisions. It would be helpful, though, for you to take the time to learn about all the current brands and what they may offer that can meet your needs. You can do this by keeping your eyes open when you are on the internet and when you read a magazine or newspaper. When you are looking at what's for sale on websites, take a sweeping look. Look and listen to learn about all the brands and kinds of high-tech devices you may be interested in, so you have the big picture and can put your favorite into perspective relative to other devices.

Key Word

A **smart tablet** is a wireless, portable personal computer. It is flat, with a touchscreen interface, and is typically larger than a smartphone and smaller than a laptop computer. Examples are the Apple iPad and the Microsoft Surface. In this book, "smart tablet" refers to all brands of smart tablets.

Watch Out for the Bleeding Edge

Should you rush to buy the instant something new and exciting is announced? Should you stand in line to be the first person on your block or among your friends to have it? Maybe. But realize that the first model of any new technological marvel may have some technical problems, some or all of which get worked out over time.

Consider the case of the Samsung Galaxy Note 7

What about Upgrades?

When should you upgrade to a new product? That's a personal decision, depending on how much you want the new features, how exciting those features are in contrast to what you already have, how much the upgrade will cost, and how much of your personal time it will take to upgrade to the new product.

Think about how you decide to buy a new car rather than driving your old one for another year. Do you want the higher reliability of a newer car that doesn't need to go into the shop as often or unexpectedly, the improved safety features and handling, better fuel economy, additional functionality with improved navigation that will help avoid traffic jams, and new kinds of entertainment and other capabilities? Do you want the sleeker design, the new car smell (is that a good thing, with all the new materials outgassing right into our noses)? Do you want a newer car that works better with other high-tech gadgets, including smartphones that have more capability and batteries that last longer? Do you want an electric plug-in vehicle that goes further on each battery charge? You will have to make a judgment on upgrades based on your personal needs and preferences.

Key Word

Bleeding edge technology has been defined as "technology that is far ahead of the cutting edge of consumer acceptance."[214] Sometimes, ultra-new technology is rushed to market without sufficient testing, especially the software, which is a key component of almost all new technology.[215] Sometimes, the technology itself is unreliable.

smartphone, introduced in mid-August 2016. Within the first two weeks, it experienced at least 35 explosions and fires involving its lithium ion battery, mostly while charging.[16] Samsung finally joined the US Consumer Product Safety Commission warning consumers to stop using these smartphones immediately. Samsung ceased manufacturing them and issued a worldwide recall.[17]

Reliability specialists have a term for product failure behavior that may apply here. It's called the "bathtub curve," and it shows a lot of devices failing very early in their life, called "infant mortality."[18] Devices are then stable until they gradually start wearing out near end of their life. If a product is new on the market, it may experience infant mortality or other early reliability issues. It may also have been rushed to market without enough testing, and the hardware may have glitches or, more likely, the software may not yet be ready for prime time. Assuming the device has been designed to be updatable, new versions of the software can be downloaded through the internet or loaded in some other way.

You will have to judge based on your personal experience, your excitement level for something new, and the available information about a new high-tech gadget as to whether you want to jump right in or wait for a while. Waiting at least a little while will let things settle down on the manufacturing and support front, with early kinks being ironed out so the device you buy has a higher likelihood of working well. You will also have the advantage of having access to reviews of early users' experiences, which may reinforce your interest in the new gadget or help you decide to wait for the next model.

Many people are proud of being "early adopters" of new technological things. They are willing to stand in long lines in the middle of the night to be the first on their block to have them.[19] Very early adopters have something in their blood that gives them a thrill to have the latest, newest thing before anyone else has it. You may be one of these people. If so, my hat is off to you! But I usually wait a while to let the dust settle before jumping in with both feet. Early first adopters can get bruised from time to time if they are often at the bleeding edge.

Smart Tip

Sometimes it is helpful to wait a little while after a new high-tech device comes out before buying so you can read about early buyer experiences.

There is a difference, however, between very early adopters who go for truly bleeding edge technology, only to be stung some of the time, and early adopters who buy and use proven technology incorporated into new products or new versions of products. In the early days of PCs it became clear that if we waited a year or two, we could get a lot more for our money. It was tempting for many people to wait until they could get a better deal. But while waiting they would have no PC or would have to put up with an obsolete PC for a long time, perhaps losing personal productivity and the benefits of new functionality that could make a real difference in their lives.

I have been enamored of several bleeding-edge things; some of them never worked well and others were winners. I bought a home networking hub that has never worked well and is not particularly useful. I usually wait a bit before jumping in to buy the latest version of a smartphone or PC, giving it time to mature. I waited a while for Windows 10 to mature before upgrading to it, defying my old Windows 7 operating system's frequent encouragements to upgrade soon. I waited a while to get a video doorbell, holding off until things settled in the marketplace and I had confidence that this new type of product would meet my needs. I will probably wait to upgrade my smartphone until my old one breaks or a new one comes out that is significantly better in terms of features that are meaningful to me.

Tech Shoppers Guide

Now that you are thinking about what you really need and have done a little planning, it's time to consider what's going to happen when you go online or step into a store. Although you can just walk into a store cold, you put yourself at a disadvantage unless you intend to window shop one day and do your serious shopping later. Using Google or another search engine to research your options will help you be much better informed before you shop, and you can do your research quickly and easily. If you go to Amazon or another online shopping site first, you can get a feel for what is available, see typical prices, and read some reviews that may be helpful. You might even decide to buy online and save yourself a trip to a store.

But be careful about online shopping site reviews because some have been posted by biased sources, including individuals using assumed names. It's OK to use these reviews as part of your research, as long you also check unbiased review sites like CNET or Consumer Reports. For some types of high-tech products, such as TVs and smartphones, popular shopping and review sites, like Amazon, Best Buy, and Consumer Reports, provide point-by-point comparisons of different brands and models. Look at some of the worst reviews as well as the favorable ones to get a balanced view of buyers' experiences. Be sure to also talk with friends and colleagues about what you are thinking of purchasing, and solicit their ideas and opinions.

Preparing before you shop can help you get a better deal. When you are ready to buy, either in a store or online, be careful to buy what you intended to buy. Don't let yourself be redirected to something less familiar that you don't know much about, unless you have given full consideration to the alternative.

We can quite easily go into a store or a car dealer and have an idea of what we want. But before we know it, we begin wanting something with a lot more features and performance that we may not really need. Every time we buy something with more features, we are generally adding complexity to the

Smart Tip

Avoid being upsold: Don't buy things with features you don't really need that may add unneeded complexity and cost. Also, watch out for "bait and switch" tactics.

thing we are buying and to our lives. Salespeople are very good at "upselling," moving you up to a fancier smart TV or a car with more features. They may be motivated to do this by higher commissions or other incentives to push certain products.

So, sometimes we have to rely on the information that we have been able to find with a few Google searches and maybe an online consumer buying guide. With that, we just have to go by our gut feeling as to whether we really need additional capabilities or not.

A salesperson who doesn't give simple, straightforward answers to your questions can be a red flag signaling that you should not rush into a purchase until you have the information you need.

Smart Tip

Ask lots of questions about new, high-tech things you are considering. Do not be shy or embarrassed because you don't know precise technical terminology.

The salesperson should be able to talk about the product's features and strong and weak points. So, ask why one device is better than another. Ask whether the salesperson has tried the device. Do they own one like it? What does the salesperson like about it? Ask how the device the salesperson seems to be favoring compares to one or two other ones. If the answers are vague or long-winded, you may be hearing "salesperson bluster," and it may not be helpful to you.

You may also be able to find answers to your questions

with just a little research on the web or by asking a friend. Don't forget to ask yourself questions, too, about what you need. Is the product you are considering well-matched to your needs? Is it fast enough, and is it easy to use? If you feel rushed into deciding while you are in a store, consider backing off and leaving, and then come back later or go to another store when you may be more knowledgeable and may get a more responsive salesperson. Do not be rushed into buying!

Smart Tip

Take a breath! Back off and leave and come back later. You may get a better deal, and you most likely will have thought through the decision better and be more informed. Be suspicious about deals that a salesperson says are good only "right now" or "today only"!

To the extent possible, keep an open mind about your high-tech options, even if you immediately fall in love with the sleekest, fastest car, smartphone, or other high-tech device the moment you see it. Play a little hard to get, with the salesperson and with yourself. Be sure before you buy!

Here's another observation you should consider as you shop for new high-tech things. Often, products that employ the latest technology cost less than older versions because they cost less to make. Mass production using new technology can also lead to the inclusion of features that you may not need along with those you really do need, sometimes at no extra cost. For example, that high-resolution TV screen may come only as part of a smart TV. You may have to buy the smart TV, then consider not using some of its features if you don't want them. Look at Chapter 9, "How To Survive New Technology," for a discussion about the possible loss of privacy if you leave certain smart TV features enabled.

Buying high-tech things can be fun, but doing a little homework before you buy puts you ahead of the curve. You have more knowledge, and you can develop a strategy for getting the best buy. Just dial back your high-tech euphoria a bit so logic can prevail in the buying process. And don't rush into buying something unless you need it urgently.

In the next chapter, you will learn about some of the downsides of new technology. As you prepare to buy and use all these new high-tech devices, it will be helpful to hear some cautionary tales about people who aren't convinced that new technology is the greatest thing since sliced bread. You will also find out more about some of the pitfalls of new technology and how you can avoid them.

Key Points

- We usually shop for newer technology with all the bells and whistles.
- We buy things that meet our needs, but we are also influenced by ads and recommendations from friends.
- It helps to put emotions aside and use logic in the purchase process. It's OK to have preferences, such as brands you like because you are familiar with them and things you like because they have worked well for you in the past. But be careful about bleeding edge things that may not be ready for prime time.
- It helps to plan your purchase, thinking about what you want to buy, what features you need, and narrowing your options. Give special attention to whether you are ready for an upgrade or if what you have now may still meet your needs.
- Do a little preparation for buying by searching on the web, reading some reviews, and getting opinions from friends and colleagues.
- Be careful whether you buy online or in a store. Focus on what you want and resist being upsold or pushed to an alternative product that may not meet your needs as well.

CHAPTER 3

DOWNSIDES OF NEW TECHNOLOGY

WHILE WE ARE ON our technology high, it is helpful to consider a few cautionary thoughts about adverse effects that new technology can introduce. This may help us put our enthusiasm in perspective and could be called watching out for the thorns among the roses. Some of these downsides affect individuals primarily, and some are broader concerns. You can mitigate some of these downsides by following the "Smart Tips" and other strategies in this chapter.

Downsides Affecting Individuals

Let's first examine the downsides of technology that affect individuals. From a trend toward relating more to our high-tech devices than to our friends and colleagues to losing our ability to reason, remember, and focus, technology is changing us — and not always for the better.

Relating More to Technology Than to People

Are we relating more to technology than to other people? Maybe. We would rather use an ATM than wait in line to talk with a teller at a bank. We prefer to check ourselves out at a grocery store rather than stand in line for a clerk to ring things up and bag groceries for us. We say it's faster, and it often is. But we may be making that choice because we don't really want to chat with the teller or clerk. We sometimes prefer to chat with our technological things rather than with people we don't know.

But what happens when we avoid people more and more and while we interact more and more with our smartphones and ATMs and automated gas pumps and other high-tech inanimate things? What happens when we walk around with our noses to our smartphones, ignoring people around us? Some of us are beginning to lose our social skills, our ability to talk to and work amicably with other people. People were already in danger when they started watching hours of TV rather than interacting with family and other people. Now, the danger is much greater, and the effects may not fall just on the individuals involved, but on society as a whole, as people disengage from other people often and, sometimes, for long periods of time, preferring to substitute technology for companionship. Banks and retailers encourage us to disengage from people by installing ATMs, automated gas pumps, and self-checkout lines in grocery stores because it saves them money when we help ourselves rather than rely on tellers or retail cashiers.

We can spend hours using our smartphones, laptops, and PCs, without realizing how much time has gone by. As we have fun watching online videos or hanging out on social media, however, we are not talking with or observing people around us. As we disappear into the technology cocoon, we become disconnected from the real world. We begin to become antisocial as we relate more to technology than to people.

Becoming Too Dependent on Technology

Another concern about new technology is that the more we depend on it, the less we can do for ourselves. We rely so much on technological devices that we may become more dependent on the gadgets and less on our minds and bodies for creature comforts as well as extravagances.

Smart Tip

Try to balance your life a bit by taking the time to put down your smartphone and talk to people every so often.

Are we losing our ability to function as human beings because new technology has become so much of a crutch and we have become so dependent on it that we are "lesser persons" than we were in the past?[20] We can already see that we tend to search online for things rather than remembering them.[21] For example, people tend to look up addresses and phone numbers repeatedly, whenever they need them, rather than memorizing them.

Have you found that it is now more difficult to remember phone numbers because you depend on your smartphone to remember for you? You just press a name in your contact list and—*voilà!*—your phone dials the number automatically. Have you ever been in a panic when you didn't have your smartphone with you and urgently needed your spouse's or your children's phone numbers, which you could no longer remember without your smartphone? How many phone numbers do you have committed to memory? We don't really want to remember phone numbers. Why clutter our precious short-term human memory with things we don't need to know?

But it's possible that we are losing something precious that we once had, such as the ability to recall instantly the phone numbers of family and close friends. Maybe our brains have lost some of their short- or long-term memory capability because they are not being exercised enough to be able to carry out these functions well. Is the same thing happening to our basic computational ability, too? When is the last time a cashier calculated your change rather than relying on an automated cash register to determine how much change to return to you? Why remember how to do arithmetic if it is done automatically for us many times each day? You could carry this one step further by questioning why we should learn arithmetic in the first place, but after saying this, it becomes clear that if we can't do the math we are at the mercy of technology and other people, and we wouldn't be able to function fully in the world when we need to.

Our minds may be changing as we let our iPhone or our PC repeatedly do things for us. When we use popular software like TurboTax or Tax ACT, we are giving up a personal understanding of the reasoning behind what we owe in taxes to our computer or to the web rather than understanding how things are calculated. We are losing our ability to discover mistakes or to know the assumptions that have been made in preparing our taxes. Why worry about how things work or whether they work right when we can live without cluttering our minds with these details?

Maybe we only notice something might be wrong when things don't work as expected. That's when we begin to wonder what's going on under the hood, so to speak, and whether our technology is doing the right thing. But we shouldn't wait for our tech to go awry. We should be able to do basic calculations by hand to make sure they are being done correctly for us by a cash register or a PC, or even by complicated income tax software. Review a receipt in a restaurant or a store to make sure it contains the right items and the numbers generally add up. Calculating the tax is another story, since you must know the state and maybe the local tax rates that apply to what you are buying.

Perhaps even worse than not being able to remember phone numbers or make change is our tendency to email or

Smart Tip

Exercise your mind by checking your bills at restaurants and stores to make sure they are correct. And be sure to count your change, too, if you pay by cash.

text rather than make a phone call or visit someone in person. New technology has made our lives less personal and may have interfered with our ability to be the social animals we were just a few decades ago. We may have begun to withdraw from society and retreat into our high-tech cave as we depend on technology to take care of us.

Smart Tip

Occasionally, make a phone call instead of emailing or texting. Your family, friends, and others will appreciate it . . . probably.

Conforming to Technology

As computers are embedded in just about everything around us, we begin to wonder about what happened to our comfortable old appliances and electronic devices that were so easy to use. User interfaces on new devices often seem awkward and hard to use. Sometimes, these interfaces give the impression that the computer is in charge—and we better do what it says. The computer-based device may be encouraging us to be more productive, move faster, and do things in a structured way, all of which is determined by the computer, not by us. This is happening on the factory floor, where humans sometimes help robotic arms and other devices do their job, such as feeding them parts and doing other supportive tasks. Both robots and humans are being monitored by computer-based control systems that are intended to increase productivity and improve quality.

This is happening elsewhere in the workplace, too. Consider what is happening to our primary care doctors as they are forced to use electronic record-keeping systems that seem to do more than keep records. Doctors appear to be spending as much time communing with their PCs or laptops as they do with their patients. In this process, the record-keeping system sometimes seems to be leading the doctor along in using the system, even in diagnosing a patient's illness. This could interfere with the doctor's ability to use their judgment to diagnose the patient. These systems were "sneaked" into the doctor's office in the name of HIPAA, ensuring the privacy of patient information, but they sometimes lead a doctor by the nose to collect patient symptoms, lab test results, and other data. They may prompt the doctor about which questions to ask the patient to elicit still more data before the system attempts to assist the doctor in a diagnosis.[22] Automation may also significantly decrease a doctor's productivity, since physicians may be able to see only a fraction of the patients they could see just a few years earlier because the computer programs demand so much time.

To some extent, computers are even beginning to take charge in the home.[23] Home automation devices like thermostats and lights are set up by homeowners to enable computer-controlled devices to turn lights on and off following a set schedule. The thermostat is programmed to prepare the house for nighttime and morning. The video doorbell informs us when someone approaches the front door or when they ring the doorbell, expecting us to interrupt what we are doing to respond to its alerts, even if we aren't home.

We are being pushed to conform to the world according to the computer. We are losing flexibility. We are being forced to be predictable so our computer-based assistants can support us better, because they are somewhat limited when it comes to flexibility. We must use the right words to talk to the car navigation system so it (he or she…) can understand us. We then must put up with unnatural action sequences and with stilted attempts to speak English back to us. The navigation system is likely to speak some techno-babble, too. It uses the language of the techies who created it, without adequate input from experts in human-computer interface design or enough feedback from real users who have tried to use the system.

We must learn to push back on technology when it gets too intrusive and tries to take charge. To do that, we must be aware that we may be, little by little, giving up control some of the time. Then, we can take steps to be sure we are in charge when we want to be, to stick up for ourselves when we sense that we should. This is a wiser move than giving in by default to the technology and the "system" around us at home, work, or elsewhere that may be encroaching on our prerogatives as humans.

Decreased Ability to Read in Depth

As exciting as it is to read articles and books on our smartphones, smart tablets, PCs, laptops, and ebook readers, some experts are concerned that we are losing something of value when we read this way.[24] They observe that people tend to scan and skim when reading on an electronic medium rather

Smart Tip

Be prepared to push back on technology when it threatens to take over too much of your life. Find ways to rely less on technology to achieve a balance between you controlling it and it controlling you. Just like with pushy people, you may have to exert yourself to have the last word.

than on old fashioned paper. It has been suggested that we are losing our ability to read in depth, analyze, infer, and think new thoughts. The process of reading has changed, and the results of our reading may have changed as well — maybe for the worse — due to our superficial reading habits.

One summary of this trend, by cognitive neuroscientist Maryanne Wolf, concludes that "the new norm in reading is skimming, word spotting, and browsing on a screen. Rather than reading in a linear sequential manner, people read in a zigzag fashion. They skim, read a little, and skim some more."[25] Wolf says that people shift their attention more than 20 times an hour while using digital devices. Skimming while reading is a good thing to do when you are scanning to find something or trying to get the big picture. But if you never dig deeper into the text, giving it your full attention, you may be missing a lot of the content and not fully understanding it, especially the subtleties.

Separation Anxiety

A study by the University of Missouri concludes that the effects of being separated from our smartphones are both psychological and physiological, including poor performance on

Is Technology Moving Too Fast?

In the name of progress, are we being forced to give up last year's technology so we can keep up with this year's new and improved technology? An Edelman Trust Barometer report says that "a 27-country survey measuring confidence in the public and private sectors found that the majority of the world's consumers think technological change is moving too fast for them."[216] This report says that "technology for technology's sake, most people feel, is not a good thing." I suppose that many people feel that some of the new technology has resulted from techies creating new technology because it is fun to do, instead of listening to what people want and need. Are some of these technical folks jerking us around so they can have fun and so their companies can make more money?

Many people who have these types of concerns become cautious adopters of new technology rather than early adopters. Some of them, particularly older folks, may drag their feet, trying to live with older technology that supports their basic needs. They may not even be aware of how much the newer technology could improve their lives.

Key Word

An **ebook reader** is a mobile electronic device that is designed primarily for the purpose of reading digital ebooks and periodicals. Sometimes we can use a general purpose smart tablet to read ebooks, too.

cognitive tests.[26] The results "suggest that smartphones are capable of becoming an extension of our selves such that when separated from them we experience a lessening of 'self' and a negative physiological state."[27] In other words, we can develop smartphone separation anxiety. These researchers also found a drop in cognitive performance and a jump in blood pressure, heart rate, and overall anxiety when peoples' smartphones were not nearby.

Another study, which was based on research in the UK and Hong Kong and reported in the British newspaper *The Guardian*, gave cell phone separation anxiety a name: "No-mophobia, or no-mobile phobia."[28] Other sources use this term for the anxiety people experience when their smartphone battery is running low.[29]

New Technology Can Be Fragile

More than one cable TV company representative has told their customers, "I'm sorry, but you'll have to unplug the set-top box, wait 10 seconds, and plug it back in again." Why? Nobody knows. In fact, it's not clear what the problem is or what caused it. These issues happen so often that it's safe to say that our personal technological infrastructure is somewhat fragile, which can try our patience.

This kind of fragility can make life difficult when we become dependent on devices that don't work all the time. Frequently, we just have to live with it, sometimes adapting our lives to how the product works. A new, high-tech device can stop working correctly for a range of reasons. The culprit could be some internal issue, a problem with another device it is connected to, or the result of a cyberattack. Make sure you have backed up the data on your PCs, smartphones, and similar devices to the cloud or external storage. Check out the "Smart Tips" in the next chapter about backing up your data.

Beware of Becoming a Tech Hoarder

Another concern as we rush out to buy every new tech gizmo that comes on the market is tech hoarding. Do you always sell, donate, or recycle your old electronics when you buy new things? Many people don't, and this can lead to boxes of old electronic gear around the house. It can also lead you to try to keep an older device going at the same time you are learning to use a new one, possibly distracting you and making it harder to get familiar with the new one. Your focus needs to be on becoming familiar with your new high-tech devices so you can get the most out of them.

Cleaning out the clutter from your home—and mind—can have other advantages. For not quite-so-old electronics, such as 2-year-old smartphones, there is a lucrative resale market. In other cases, such as for older TVs with cathode ray tubes (CRTs), you may have to pay to recycle old electronics, but it may be worth it to help you focus on new things.

I'm not completely cold-hearted. It can be nostalgic to keep a few select pieces of old gear, such as my original Mac and a few old vinyl records that reside in my basement, along with a turntable to play them on. For the record, I sold my original IBM PC several years ago, and I had mixed feelings about parting with it.

What happens if the power goes out and our uninterruptable power supply (UPS) battery runs down? Should we consider buying an emergency generator for the future, or is that overkill? What happens if the battery runs down on our smartphone and the power is out so we can't charge it? Should we have an external battery backup, just in case? Lots of people do. I recently experienced a 24-hour Fios outage that the Verizon technician said was caused by a broken optical fiber a block or so from my home. We either have to compensate for this fragility by being prepared with backups or decide that planning for these kinds of problems is not worth it to us.

Smart Tip

Determine your tolerance level for high-tech devices to run out of battery power or to fail in some other way. Then, decide what kind of backup you need and how much, like an uninterruptable power supply for your PC and Wi-Fi router. You might want to consider a second smartphone, just in case.

Exposure to Radiation

There are continuing concerns about radiation from electrical things around us, including smartphones which we may hold close to our heads and wearable devices that are close to our body much of the time. But there still appears to be no definitive evidence that this kind of exposure to radiation will result in long-term harm to us.[30]

However, the coast isn't entirely clear. The blue light from the LED screens on our smartphones, PCs, and TVs is a form of radiation. Our extensive use of devices with LED screens can confuse our pineal gland.[31] The pineal gland is in our brain, and it makes melatonin, a hormone that regulates sleep. The effect is especially troublesome for teenagers, resulting in loss of sleep and confusion of body rhythms through the night and beyond. To help counter this effect, iPhones and other devices now have an optional capability to decrease the amount of blue light as nightfall approaches so we can get a better night's sleep.

Smart Tip

Consider turning down the blue light on your smartphone as bedtime approaches, perhaps with an automatic setting so you don't have to think about it. You may sleep better!

New Technology May Lead to Unemployment

Consider what happens when new technology is introduced on the factory floor. Over the last few decades, the introduction of robots and other forms of automation in the manufacturing sector have led to more output per hour of labor, and thus, a rise in productivity. At the same time, many manufacturing jobs requiring less-skilled workers have disappeared, and newer, higher-level jobs have been created. Over the short term, some people lose their jobs when automation is introduced, but, in the past, after workers are retrained, there have generally been enough jobs for everyone. Workers are now often trained at the beginning of their careers to work in partnership with the new technology.

This process has been going on for years. It led well-known economist John Maynard Keynes to coin the term "technological unemployment" in the 1930s.[32] And President John F. Kennedy declared that the major domestic challenge of the 1960s was to "maintain full employment at a time when automation is replacing men."[33]

But, recently, economists have disagreed as to whether the introduction of certain types of technology will lead to long-term increased unemployment. MIT economist David Autor thinks this long-term employment stability may be changing, starting in about 2000, when there was a "great sag in employment." The Center for Business and Economic Research reports that the US lost about 5.6 million manufacturing jobs between 2000 and 2010, 85 percent of them attributable to technological change.[34] The Center found that the manufacturing sector has become more productive and industrial output has been growing during this period. *Bloomberg Businessweek* reported that "technology's influence (on productivity) is hard to predict."[35] Banks, retailers, and other companies used information technology from 1995 to 2004 to contribute to an increase in output per hour for US businesses at a 3 percent annual pace during the decade. But in the same *Bloomberg Businessweek* article, Robert Gordon, a professor at Northwestern University, is quoted as saying, "The fruits of the third industrial revolution [information technology] may be coming to an end."

As more than a symbol of the limits of our human capabilities, remember that robots can work 24 hours a day, except for a little maintenance now and then, while we usually only put in eight hours or so each day. Robert J. Samuelson, a *Washington Post* journalist and former magazine columnist, puts this in perspective by observing that automation creates services and expands consumer choice.[36] It also eliminates some people's jobs, though. But there is hope, since Samuelson also notes that "someone has to design, program, service, and coordinate the robots and other digitized processes."

So, there is a glimmer of hope for people in lower-level

jobs, especially for those who are willing to be trained in newer, higher-level jobs. But humans in higher-level jobs have reason for concern, too. W. Brian Arthur, a visiting researcher at the Xerox Palo Alto Research Center and a former Stanford economics professor, says that "digital versions of human intelligence" are increasingly replacing even those jobs once thought to require people."[37] Technology is gradually eating its way up the food chain of highly skilled jobs, even beginning to impinge on lawyers, architects, doctors, and others who perform work that requires high intelligence, extensive training, education, and experience. This frequently takes the form of technology taking over somewhat menial tasks, such as lawyers searching through law periodicals and doctors seeking information in the latest medical journals, in addition to interpreting X-rays and other diagnostic imaging results. But watch out: Some existing technology can perform some medical diagnosis and architectural design, as well as other high-level functions.

The jury is out as to the effect of new technology on jobs. The jobs built on the use of new technology may result in higher productivity for individual workers and companies, and for the economy at large. This may all result in dislocations in the workforce that could last a while. In the past, most individuals have eventually found a new job, and, overall, our standard of living became higher. Let's hope that this pattern continues in the future, especially when our technology becomes smarter and jobs that require greater knowledge and higher skill levels become threatened.

We Are Driven to Distraction

Let's consider another downside of new technology. Why do some people use phones while driving, when doing so may seriously harm themselves or others? How many times do we have to be warned about talking on the phone while driving before we realize that it's dangerous to talk on a phone and drive? Analyses have shown that it is as dangerous to drive while talking on a cell phone, even hands-free, as it is to drive while intoxicated![38] The American Automobile Association has reported that distraction by phones and other things is worst among teenage drivers, with distraction a factor in 58 percent of crashes.[39]

The National Safety Council has summarized many of the concerns about distracted driving from a number of studies.[40] According to the Council, driving while talking on a cell phone creates inattention blindness (where we are not really processing everything in our field of view as we drive), leads to slower response and reaction times, and makes it harder for drivers to stay in the proper lane. The Council estimates that 21 percent of all car crashes involve the use of a cell phone while driving. The *Washington Post* published a summary of a study by Cambridge Mobile Telematics that found "in nearly a quarter of crashes the driver was using a phone within a minute before the crash occurred, and perhaps even at the moment of the crash."[41] The *New York Times* cited a study commissioned by AT&T that found "6 percent of people admitted they text while driving, 33 percent said they email, and 27 percent said they use Facebook."[42]

Perhaps even worse than talking while driving is texting while driving. The Virginia Tech Transportation Institute has reported that the collision risk when drivers were distracted by texting was 23 times greater than when not texting![43] This problem may get worse as car manufacturers collaborate with smartphone makers to have texts appear on the dashboard or, even worse, projected onto the windshield.

Always Watching, Always Listening

New technology all around us has resulted in cameras and

Smart Tip

Don't text while driving! Minimize your use of your cell phone to talk, too. Even hands-free use is risky. Your driving behavior under the influence of cell phone use can be just as bad as if you had been drinking!

microphones being used to watch and listen to us—wherever we are. Other things around us are tracking much of what we do every day, too. Let's start with the obvious things first.

Cameras and Microphones Are Everywhere

Is there no place that's sacred anymore? We are on camera when we are at home and work, while driving or walking or sitting in our favorite coffee shop. Every day the news includes stories of people being observed on camera on the street, in buildings, and in elevators. We are on camera on highways and toll roads, and license plates are sometimes scanned while our car is in a parking garage or parked on the side of the road. And don't forget about the red light and speed cameras that take pictures of drivers, cars, and license plates. The *Washington Post* has reported that there is a privately maintained database of license plate numbers scanned by cameras used by police, parking garages, and others in the US, and this database is being used by many organizations, including the Department of Homeland Security, for law enforcement, tracking immigrants, and other purposes.[44] London, England, has been at the forefront of surveillance, with cameras and microphones all over the place to help police respond to terrorism and other crimes. If you drive into central London, your license plate will be scanned as part of the city's crime prevention effort and to send you a bill to discourage you from entering the congested, central part of London.

Why are we on camera so often? Cameras and other sensors on local roads and highways help authorities manage traffic, detecting backups in time to alleviate major traffic tie-ups. Homeowners have posted cameras for years as part of their security systems, but video doorbells like Ring and Doorbot have suddenly joined a growing legion of what some see as visible deterrents to crime and others view as an invasion of privacy in peaceful neighborhoods. Retail stores, banks, and other places of business commonly use theft-deterrent interior and exterior cameras.

To illustrate the extent of the cameras around us, consider the horrific 2013 Boston Marathon bombing, where a network of cameras on city streets was used to identify the culprits in action and to prosecute them. This video evidence was collected from many separate and independent video security cameras.[45] In some urban areas, there are also arrays of microphones that detect gunshots and pinpoint their location.[46]

Google has vehicles with cameras on top of them that drive by homes across the US and elsewhere in the world, taking "street view" pictures of houses that sometimes include pictures of people and cars. For a two-year period, the Google cars taking these pictures also recorded Wi-Fi locations and data signals when the data wasn't encrypted.[47] How many people with Wi-Fi routers know that the signal can extend to nearby streets? This is one good reason to make sure encryption is turned on. Encrypting the signal also prevents cyberattackers from using the Wi-Fi to attack PCs and smartphones and other devices connected to it. See Chapter 4 for cybersecurity tips about setting up your Wi-Fi.

Tracking Us Is Easy with Credit Cards and More

We leave a trail of credit card transactions every day. We use credit card systems at stores, restaurants, and online that create permanent records of what, when, and where we buy things. ATMs track our cash withdrawals and other bank transactions, timestamping everything, and even including video of us using the ATM. We also use readable electronic keys to gain access to hotel rooms, office buildings, and other areas, leaving a record of our movements as we use them.

We can also be tracked and monitored through our smartphones, sometimes when they aren't even on. Hackers can set a smartphone so the microphone is always on, even when the smartphone is turned off, sending the sounds around the phone to the hackers.[48] Some Voice over IP (VoIP) landline phones can be hacked so their microphones are turned on all the time, sending the audio from an office or home to the hackers, wherever they are on the internet.[49] We can also be monitored by GPS-based fitness trackers that report how we are doing and where we are to a server in the cloud. And retailers can send advertising texts or emails for specials on a particular aisle by detecting where we are in the store via our cell phones.

When we use Google Maps for navigation, Google tracks our location, collecting location information from our smartphone and from the smartphones of other cars driving on our route.[50] It uses this information in Google Maps to tell us about traffic jams we might want to avoid.

Our Cars Are Getting in on the Act Too

We can also be tracked by car navigation systems that can share information with Google, car manufacturers, or others about where we are (using GPS and other means), where we are going, and where we have been. Almost all cars have maintenance connectors, known as onboard diagnostics

Key Word

Voice over IP (VoIP) landline phones use Internet Protocol (IP) to transmit digital data in small chunks, called "packets," on the internet. The Internet Protocol establishes some of the rules for formatting, transmitting, and receiving data through a network. Landline phones are the old fashioned phones that are attached to wires, which are still used in some homes and in many offices.

Key Word

GPS stands for **Global Positioning System**, which is a global system of satellites and satellite receivers that enables the accurate location of our smartphones, cars, airplanes, and other things.

Key Word

The **cloud** is a name for large aggregations of computers and data storage on the internet, usually in large data centers. We use the cloud to store data and perform computations to support high-tech devices in our home and elsewhere. We don't know where these computers in the cloud are located. We only know that they are "out in the cloud."

(OBD) ports, that can be used to detect and diagnose vehicle malfunctions. Sometimes these ports also provide access to a car's event data recorder, or "black box." Information that can be gleaned from these black boxes includes the last several seconds of data before an accident, which may indicate the car's speed and whether the brakes were applied and if seatbelts were worn.[51]

When you use highway toll systems with transponders, you can be tracked where you are and when, which means the operators of these systems know how fast you went from one toll point to another. Another big-brother development on the car front is the inclusion of cameras inside some newer cars, sometimes aimed at the driver. Driver-facing cameras can track a driver's eyes to make sure the driver is not distracted or becoming drowsy.[52] Cadillac and Nissan use this capability to ensure that drivers using assisted-driving tools continue to pay attention. *Consumer Reports* states that the Tesla Model 3 has a camera just above the rearview mirror that is aimed at the car's occupants. Tesla can apparently activate that camera through new software releases, and the company says they will notify Model 3 owners when the camera is activated.

You Aren't Alone If You Are Online

We are being spied on in a different way when we use our smartphones and PCs to search the web for data, send email, or use apps. Google search and Gmail are "free," but the content of every search is being saved and used by Google for commercial purposes, such as steering ads to us based on what we search. Google also employs data from Google Maps and YouTube to help steer ads to customers. Responding to increasing public concern about privacy, Google has implemented a "pause" option so users can prevent Google from collecting data from their web activity, and location and YouTube history.

Apple also stores data about us. It has revamped its privacy policy to tell its customers that "it is not interested in their personal data, even as it must use more of that data to deliver personalized products."[53] Apple says "we don't 'monetize' the information you store on your iPhone or in the iCloud." But Facebook has been in the news as the public has become aware of how it does monetize its users' personal information, even providing tools that have enabled what the company called "malicious actors" to discover the identities and collect information on most of its 2 billion users.[54] According to Facebook, these malicious actors were the people who initiated a cyberattack on the site, in part using tools then built into the Facebook platform, to steal users' email addresses and phone numbers.

Key Word

A **cyberattack** is an attempt by criminals, or "hackers" who are just having fun, or even foreign governments, to steal or change data or to damage or destroy a computer system or network.

We can also be tracked doing other things online. For example, when we read news online, using our smartphone or PC, the news website may be able to discern and record political and other preferences by knowing which news stories we read and in what order. When we visit websites, they know what smartphone or PC we are using to access them, and, in general, where we are and what website we visited before we connected to their site.

Siri can listen all the time for your "Hey, Siri" command. Or she can be set to listen only after the push of a button on the iPhone. When talking to Siri, you may think you are just talking to your iPhone, but you are speaking to Apple, in the cloud, and the response is from the Apple cloud, too. Are your questions to Siri kept forever in the Apple cloud? They just may be . . . for research purposes, of course, to improve how Siri performs in the future. In fact, one of the research areas for personal assistants like Siri is to have responses to our questions build on the entire stream of previous inquiries, as well as everything else Apple knows about us. Using this information may help Siri to give us a better answer, in the context of our personal history.

Apple has extended Siri so she (or he, if you like . . . there's a setting for that) can connect to the Apple HomeKit home automation system, as well as Apple's streaming music service, called Apple Music.[55] Apple has also put Siri in the Apple Watch and in a version of the Apple TV.

For Windows 10 users, Microsoft has created a personal assistant named Cortana.[56] Users can ask Cortana questions, just like Siri, by talking into a microphone on the PC or laptop or by typing. Cortana can tell jokes and display the latest NBA scores, as well as set up and change calendar events. And, like Siri, the system can be set so it is always waiting to be activated when it hears the words, "Hey Cortana."

Our Homes Are the New Hacker Frontier

The Amazon Echo, Echo Dot, and Echo Spot with their Alexa personal assistant, does some of the same things as Siri does for iPhone users, and additional capabilities are being added every week or so. It is a smart speaker that is "always listening" and prepared to respond to requests from users unless the microphone is turned off using a button on top of the device. The Echo's repertoire of capabilities is growing and now includes providing traffic information among many other "skills," as Amazon calls them. It records in the Amazon cloud everything you say, just the way you said it, as a digital audio recording. Amazon has said that it keeps everything you have said to Alexa, unless you ask it to delete the recordings, which it warns "may degrade your Alexa experience."[57] Even if you request that the recordings be deleted, Amazon apparently keeps transcripts of the recordings "forever." Google has a family of personal assistants called Google Assistant, Google Now, and Google Home. Google's assistants generally use all the information you have ever put into a Google search or into an email using Gmail. Google has recently admitted that its contractors listen to recordings of people using the Google virtual assistant "to better understand language differences."[58]

In homes, there are an increasing number of things that watch and listen. Cameras in smart TVs can be turned on without a user's knowledge. TVs can report what is being watched to the manufacturer and to marketing organizations, resulting in TV watchers being bombarded by ads online and elsewhere.[59] This type of monitoring, sometimes described as "spying," has led to successful legal action against one TV manufacturer in at least one case.[60] There have been successful cyberattacks in which stalkers have turned on video cameras on laptops and smartphones without the user's knowledge, invading the user's personal privacy.[61]

A Samsung Smart TV can be always listening and watching, too, unless these functions are turned off. That's the way it can respond to the "Hi TV" command to turn the TV on and to respond to hand gestures to initiate TV functions. The TV's settings can be changed to turn off the microphone, which should work — unless it is hacked by a cyberattacker who is able to change the settings. The camera can also be turned off, but physically placing tape over the camera is a more reliable method. The camera is usually located at the center top of the TV. Look for a little hole for the camera to peek through, and cover the hole.

A function called "automatic content recognition" can be turned off as well, which can eliminate ads being sent to you based on what you are watching. Changing settings is supposed to turn these intrusive functions off, but each setting must be reviewed and changed during what is usually a complicated setup process.[62] The only foolproof way to ensure that you are not being watched or monitored from afar is to disconnect the TV from the internet. In doing so, it is important to ensure that both hardwired and Wi-Fi connections are disabled.

Signals from internet-connected baby monitors can be intercepted, and the video and sound can be used for nefarious purposes.[63] The Barbie Hello Doll listens to what a child says and sends audio through the internet to a company selected by the manufacturer to interpret the communication and send a "personal" response from the talking Barbie![64] The Barbie Hello Doll folks (Mattel) say they will let parents listen to the conversation between a child and "Barbie" . . . after the fact. This does sound scary, doesn't it!

Perhaps just as intrusive are smart electric meters that record home electricity use, reporting by wireless cellular connection back to the power company. Fortunately, this communication is encrypted so only the power company knows when our power consumption is higher or lower, which might indicate whether someone is at home.[65] The smart meter attached to my home is set to transmit electricity usage every 30 minutes. My home's electricity usage is available on the power company's website, and I must log in to see this data. But that still means that protection of this data from prying eyes within

Smart Tip

When you have some degree of control about the amount of surveillance around you, take steps to tone it down. Be aware of settings you can change for the cameras and microphones on your smartphones, PCs, and TVs. Don't unwittingly give up your or your family's privacy.

the power company or elsewhere is subject to the effectiveness of the website cybersecurity provided by the power company.

"Star Trek" Is Closer Than You Think

Some of us are already spending a lot of time talking to our helpful assistants like Siri, Alexa, and Cortana. It won't be long before we begin having "Star Trek"-like experiences, which some people have called "ambient computing." Ambient computing is when our high-tech helpers are always listening and ready to help.[66] If you happen to mention that you are out of milk, before you know it, milk is on the shopping list and may even be ordered and on the way to your house. I suppose many of these new, always-on assistants will soon be considered members of the family, so maybe we don't have to worry about the privacy implications! But what happens when we forget that this new member of the family is always in the room with us and reporting what is said back to companies somewhere on the internet?

As they become more common, we are likely to become even less aware of all the sensors around us. Many of them will be so small they can be easily overlooked, and they may be incorporated into other things that we are used to seeing every day.

This isn't just playing "private eye." This is a world in which each room might have tens or hundreds of sensors, used to control the heating and air conditioning and other things to make sure we are comfortable, with just the right lighting, and able to communicate with people elsewhere and to request services. It is a world where microphones placed around a room to support conference calls might also be used to listen to and transmit speech and other sounds in the room. When Eric Schmidt was executive chairman of Google, he said at the World Economic Forum in January 2015 that "there will be so many IP addresses, so many devices, sensors, things that you are wearing, things that you are interacting with, that you won't even sense it. It will be part of your presence all the time."[67]

It is worth observing that cell phones must be in contact with the nearest cell phone tower, and sometimes more than one, in order to function. For an incoming call to reach a cell phone, the mobile cell phone provider must know where the cell phone is. So, the cell phone provider inherently knows the location of every cell phone, and as a result, the provider knows the location of every person who is carrying a cell phone. It has been reported that some cell phone providers pass cell phone location information along to other companies, too.[68] This is another way we can be tracked, wherever we are.

In the not-too-distant future, location sensing will be even more widespread. What will that look like? A visit to Bill Gates' home might be an indication. PBS reported that when a person visits Bill Gates' house they are given a little badge to wear, called an "active badge."[69] As a person wearing one of these badges moves from room to room, sensors detect who is in the room and, using this information, change the art on the electronic display panels on the walls. The badge also triggers the music, room temperature, and lighting to align with the preference of the badge-wearer. Experiments in "ubiquitous computing" at Xerox Palo Alto Research Center, where much of the personal computing technology we now take for granted was invented, took a similar active-badge approach in the 1980s.[70] Experimental wall displays in conference rooms adapted to individuals' preferences and needs.

Key Word

Ubiquitous means something is present everywhere, like fog in the morning. **Ubiquitous computing** is all around us, ready to serve us — and watch us.

A Contrarian View

There may be broader problems with new technology, even beyond the ways it can invade our personal privacy, distract us while we're driving, or entice us to relate more to high-tech devices than to people. "A contrarian view" is a broadside against technology itself. Some people are not convinced that new technology is a good thing. In the Middle Ages, these people were called Luddites.

Now, we are more tolerant of differing points of view. But there's something to be said for slowing down to smell the roses. Our fast-paced world is sometimes confusing and cluttered with new things. Maybe we should pace ourselves so we can relax more and breathe! Is meditation at odds with new technology? Or is it complementary and essential, allowing us to savor the delights new technology brings us without becoming overwhelmed by all the gadgetry?

Some people yearn for the "good old days." Do we need alarm clocks that are connected to weather and traffic reports and the thermostat? Do we need a washing machine with umpteen cycles, most of which are seldom used? Several years ago, my washing machine repairman advised me to get a new washing machine with mechanical rather than electronic controls because his customers were happier with them than with newfangled electronic ones and because the electronic controls failed more often. Perhaps he didn't appreciate my love of new technology and didn't realize I was attracted to appliances that look new, go "beep" rather than "buzz," offer lots of options, and sport a fancy digital display and controls. Maybe he just wanted to make sure I bought a washing machine that he knew how to repair!

Some people are going retro by returning to analog rather than digital products. An article in *Time* magazine reports that sales of vinyl records, paper notebooks, and old fashioned board games have grown over the last decade.[71] I find that a mix of high-tech digital and "analog," including paper and pencil and hard-copy books, journals, and magazines, works best for me when I am organizing my thoughts. And I don't think that board games have ever gone out of style. I also like a few old fashioned analog clocks around, including my grandfather clock that I have to wind every week. You don't have to go totally retro to help reduce potential adverse impacts that technology may have in your life.

This excursion into the downsides of technology is not meant to discourage you. It is intended to focus your attention on the things to watch out for, such as the need to maintain our personal relationships, even as we develop strong attachments to tech. As we depend more on technology, we also need to take adequate steps to make sure it is there when we need it, despite its fragility at times. We must pay special attention

Smart Tip

Consider introducing a little "retro" into your life to help soften the sometimes harsh and impersonal effects of the new technology we love and use so much.

to privacy, too, since many of us have been encouraged to share so much information on social media and elsewhere. In fact, so much information is being taken from us without our permission that we need to be aware of the threat and consider adjusting our behavior. We want to ensure we are comfortable with how much of our personal information is out in the open or in large databases somewhere.

Now that we have discussed some of the downsides that could interfere with our happiness as we use new technology, it is time to address the biggest downside, cybersecurity. Read on!

Key Points

- To help us put our enthusiasm about technology in perspective, it is useful to be cautious about its potential adverse effects.
- We relate more to technology than to people. We are becoming too dependent on technology and are controlled to some degree when our high-tech devices tell us what to do. Push back when you need to so you remain in charge.
- Keep your brain active. Keep reading thoroughly when you intend to, rather than just skimming or scanning, which many people are prone to do when using an ebook reader.
- New technology can seem fragile. Prepare for possible high-tech device failures. Make sure your data is backed up! Consider battery backup, even a UPS to make sure your technology is there when you need it.
- Cameras and microphones and other sensors are often watching and listening when we are outside, walking or driving, when we are at work, and even when we are at home. Change the settings on the cameras and microphones around you so you and your family don't unwittingly give up your privacy.
- Not everyone is convinced that new technology is a good thing. Have we gone overboard? Consider going retro with a few things, like vinyl records and old fashioned board games.

CHAPTER 4

WATCH OUT FOR CYBERSECURITY

ONE DOWNSIDE OF NEW technology is so much of a concern that it deserves its own chapter: cybersecurity. Reports of cybersecurity attacks are in the news so frequently that it's hard to keep track of them. We are vulnerable to these attacks because we have become so dependent on our new technology while the developers of high-tech devices have neglected to secure them adequately against cybersecurity threats.

At home and at work we should have antivirus software on our PCs. Over the last few years, this software has included broader "malware" prevention, as viruses have become only part of the threat. Cyberattackers are good at pretending to be our friend, colleague, or boss so they can successfully attack us by sending an email with an attachment or a link to a website. Opening that email or clicking on that link could result in the compromise of your PC or smartphone.

In this chapter, you will learn why cybersecurity has become such a big concern, how vulnerabilities expose our systems and networks to cyberattacks, and about the nature of cyberthreats. You will learn what actions you can take to help avoid being the victim of a cyberattack and why it is important to take reasonable steps to avoid the sometimes-catastrophic results of one. By taking just a few precautions, you can significantly improve the protection of your systems and personal data and reduce your risk that they may become compromised. This can help you avoid the potentially disastrous results of a successful cyberattack, which can include identity theft, stolen financial assets, and other losses.

A Little Background

For years many people ignored cybersecurity threats because it takes special effort to be safe from cyberattacks and people often didn't think it was worth the trouble to protect themselves. The computer scientists and engineers who designed the internet were more concerned about making it work and making it easy to use than making it secure. The programmers who created the software for our PCs, smartphones, and other high-tech devices have also focused on making devices that work well, not ones that are necessarily secure. Security has become an add-on for the internet as well as for most of the systems and software that we depend on at work and home.

We hear about cyberattacks in the news almost every day. Cyberattackers have been way too successful intruding into the networks of retailers, banks, large companies, and government agencies. Given the potential losses, you would expect that some of these companies and government agencies would have strong cybersecurity defenses that make them virtually impossible to penetrate. Unfortunately, this is not always true. Both government and the private sector have been slow to prioritize efforts to defend against cyberattacks, and most organizations are still playing catchup against cyberthreats. Federal agencies are vulnerable to attacks, reporting over 30,000 attempts to intrude in their systems in 2016.[72] There have been large losses of sensitive personal information, such as the compromise of the records of over 20 million people during attacks on the Office of Personnel Management, the Department of Energy, the State Department, and other agencies.[73]

Cyberattackers are on the offense, and they are inherently way ahead of the defense. We need to defend against every kind of attack. The "bad guys," the cyberattackers, just need one little opening to spoil our day. Yes, it is a cat and mouse game. The attackers are the clever, persistent, sneaky cats, and our systems are the mice, always susceptible to a possible attack by a pouncing cat.

Cyber Vulnerabilities

What makes our systems and networks so vulnerable to cyberattacks? Our systems become vulnerable to cyberattacks in two ways: 1) problems with the software or hardware on our PCs, smartphones, or other devices; and 2) something we do or don't do. Sometimes we click on links in incoming emails from people we don't know, and that can let a cyberattacker into our system. Sometimes we buy the latest virus detection software and keep it up to date, and that protects us. Some of the "Smart Tips" below will give you more knowledge and confidence to take the necessary steps to avoid being the victim of a cyberattack.

When it comes to problems with our system's software and hardware, everything is so complex that it is impossible to ensure it all works correctly. No practical amount of testing can demonstrate that systems will work as intended all the time. Unintentional vulnerabilities are "baked into" our systems, just waiting to be exploited by the bad guys. Errors in software that result in vulnerabilities are discovered almost every day in most software, and, sooner or later, many of them are corrected through software updates, called patches. Vulnerabilities that have not yet been identified by the good guys are known as "zero-day" vulnerabilities.

Cybersecurity vulnerabilities can be found in all kinds of software. The operating system software on PCs and

Key Word

A **zero-day vulnerability** is a flaw in software that has usually been there from the beginning but has remained unknown to anyone. It becomes a serious problem when a cyberattacker discovers it and exploits it for a cyberattack before the software developer finds and fixes it through a software patch. When a flaw is discovered, the software developer or vendor has "zero days" to fix it before the bad guys might use the flaw for cyberattacks. Sometimes, cyberattackers find the zero-day vulnerability first and software developers only learn of it after an attack has occurred.

smartphones can have hundreds of millions of lines of software code. This software is so complex that it is always prone to containing undetected vulnerabilities, no matter how much testing has been done. However, because operating system software has built in more cybersecurity protection over the last several years, many of the attacks have been directed at applications software, such as spreadsheet and web browser software, including web browser add-ons like Adobe Flash.

Smartphone apps sometimes contain vulnerabilities, especially those that have not been subjected to extensive review and testing. Apple subjects all apps to review before making them available in its app store. That makes them more dependable than Android apps, which have to support a variety of phone models from different manufacturers. Android apps can be downloaded from the "Google play" store[74] as well as from other websites.[75] Apps submitted to Google Play are reviewed for policy.[76] That said, from time to time, apps on my iPhone do crash, so Apple's mandated testing does not guarantee they will work correctly or be completely secure all the time. In fact, many of the app updates I have received for my smartphone are for "bug fixes," or error corrections.

Key Word

An **app** is a software application program, such as Facebook or email, that can be loaded onto a smartphone.

More cybersecurity vulnerabilities have been introduced as more complex software has been developed. They are caused by a combination of complex software and its sophisticated underlying hardware, combined with greater network connectivity that can increase the risk. Most cyberattacks come through the internet, but sometimes they enter a PC or laptop through a flash drive or other removable device being used to load data or programs.

Cyber Threats

The simplest cyberattacks use "off the shelf" cyberattack kits, which are readily available on the internet. More capable attackers design attack software themselves. The software that an attacker sometimes inserts in a target system is known as "malware." The hackers generally insert it into users' systems by contaminating websites that are then visited by users or through "phishing attacks," which got this label because the bad guys are "fishing" for information about you and your smartphone or PC. Phishing attacks are intended to trick people into opening an email attachment or clicking on a web link in the email. Clicking on the attachment or link may corrupt a user's PC or smartphone.

Sometimes, the phishing email is targeted at a particular person, so it is called "spear phishing." The emails are designed to look like legitimate emails from a friend, colleague, or trusted company. Phishing emails can look so fascinating or so realistic that the recipient throws caution to the wind and clicks on the attachment or link, without taking a moment to consider that it may be dangerous. "Whaling" is a phishing attack directed toward a "really big fish," like the CEO of a company or a senior government official. The emails in these attacks are frequently customized or personalized, using information that has been obtained by prior research on the prospective victim.

Some other types of cyberattacks include a password attack, in which the assailant obtains a user's password because it is weak or has been exposed in some way, and an eavesdropping attack, where the assailant observes a user's actions by breaking into a home router or a public Wi-Fi. A denial-of-service attack is one in which so many requests are sent to a server computer that it bogs down and can't respond to normal user requests. A Trojan horse attack is when a user receives new software or a link to a compromised website, and by running the software or following the link, a user's data and the device being used are compromised.

Staying Secure

This book focuses on what we can do as individuals to protect against cyberattacks targeting our smartphones, PCs, and other devices at home and at work and elsewhere. To give you more background on securing your systems and data, it will be useful to tell you a little about what large organizations do to protect their systems. Many of these organizations have large teams of knowledgeable individuals who install and monitor good cyberdefense hardware and software, often the best that has been developed. This includes software and hardware firewalls, intrusion detection systems, software that searches for unexplained changes in a system's operation, software that searches for malware, and network protection that looks for cyberattacks entering from the outside and keeps an eye out for data that looks like it is being exfiltrated, or stolen, and sent out from these systems. Systems and networks can be configured so they can be resilient to some attacks, and thus minimize the damage. All these techniques are continually a work in progress, since the bad guys, who are on offense, continue to get better over time, while the defense tries to keep up with and, sometimes, ahead of them.

In general, we don't need these kinds of sophisticated cyberdefenses on personal devices, including home PCs and smartphones. The protective software we can readily buy and use contains some of the same high-end protection features that governments and large companies use, such as antivirus

Key Word

Malware is software that has been inserted into a system or network by a cyberattacker. It enables the attacker to steal data from the system, modify the data, or cause the system to crash. Usually, malware has been inserted into a system without the owner knowing about it. It is hard, but often possible, to find and eliminate malware.

software from companies like McAfee and Symantec. This cyberdefense software, which we can easily apply to our systems, gets better every year, and, as a result, our systems become better protected, assuming we take the steps recommended here.

Practical Advice for Protecting Systems and Data

We can successfully protect our systems and data by taking a relatively small number of precautions. *The steps that we should take are summarized below, roughly in priority order in each category, beginning with what you should do first.*

Even though there is no way to be perfect defending our systems against cyberattacks, it is important to take these reasonable steps to protect systems and personal data to reduce your risk of loss through a cyberattack. Marc Goodman, in his book *Future Crimes: Everything Is Connected, Everyone Is Vulnerable, and What We Can Do About It*, concludes that we are always going to be 10 steps behind the bad guys when it comes to protecting our systems and networks against cyberattacks.[77] My experience as chief information officer (CIO) of two US federal agencies bears this out. Cyberattackers only need to find one way to get into our systems, but we need to protect against "all" ways of attacking. Diligently taking reasonable steps to protect systems and networks, including smartphones and smart tablets, can go a long way toward preventing them from being compromised.

Some people consider that taking these steps, such as using strong passwords and updating their software with the latest patches, is wasted time that harms their productivity. They may think it interferes with getting their job done. Over the long term, however, it harms productivity not to protect your systems, since a successful cyberattack can cause hours, days, or even months of lost time, coupled with possibly significant recovery expense. This head-in-the-sand attitude about basic security precautions can result in cyberattackers gaining even more of an advantage, making successful attacks more likely. Here are some of the most effective steps to take to protect systems and data.

Staying Safe Online

Use long passwords with eight or more characters that include special characters like $ or #, both upper and lowercase letters, and numbers. A simple password can easily be guessed, and cyberattackers have tools that know thousands of the most popular passwords, so it is important to use long, complex passwords to protect your data. Using a phrase as part of the password that can easily remembered is a good way to do this, such as "slicedbreadtoday" or "trainyourdragon." As

---

Smart Tip

Use long, complex passwords containing embedded phrases that help you remember them.

---

long as you don't use a single word or an obvious phrase like "mypassword," such phrases extend the length of a password, which makes it more secure and keeps the bad guys at bay.

Use different passwords for everything online, and for your PC and smartphone, your home router or gateway, your Wi-Fi, and for individual home automation devices when possible. Avoid linking logins, such as using a Facebook login for Gmail access. This is a form of using the same password for different websites and accounts, and it can increase your

Smart Tip

Use different passwords for each website and account. Be sure to use a password to limit access to your PC to authorized individuals and to limit access to laptops and other devices.

vulnerability to cyberattacks, since a successful attack on one of your devices or accounts can lead to others.

One approach to remembering many different passwords for your websites and apps is to use password manager software to keep the passwords accessible but protected. If you are the only user of your PC, you can handwrite a password list and keep it handy, in addition to placing a backup copy in a secure location. But be very careful about doing this if family members and friends can access the list. This could give them access to your online accounts, including financial accounts. Also, be alert to what a burglar might see with just a glance around your PC. Be sure not to put your passwords on sticky notes on your monitor or laptop. It goes without saying that you never use sticky notes or cheat sheets in a public or semi-public place!

Change passwords reasonably often, like every two to six months, and immediately after any kind of compromise that may have jeopardized a password. But don't change passwords so often that you are tempted to simplify the passwords to make them easier to remember. A particularly dangerous kind of password change is simply increasing the number at the end of the password by one as an "update." The Federal Trade Commission (FTC) has reported that people who know they will be forced to change their passwords often may choose weaker passwords than if they were choosing one for longer term use.[78] So if you have control over how often you modify your passwords for different websites and online services, choose stronger passwords that you change reasonably often, rather than changing them so often that you may be tempted

Smart Tip

Change passwords often but not too often.

to weaken the passwords to make the task easier.

Change the initial or default passwords on new devices or accounts as soon as you can after you buy a new device or set up a new account. It can be so easy to just use "out of the box" passwords that come with a new device, but this is one notorious way that the bad guys compromise systems and data. Be especially careful when purchasing and setting up devices like smart thermostats and video cameras. Some of these devices contain default passwords you can't change, and as a result, they can be taken over by remote cyberattackers and used to initiate attacks on your devices and network and even against other systems on the internet.

Smart Tip

Don't use default passwords.

In addition to passwords, some financial and other websites support "multifactor authentication," which can significantly improve protection from cyberattacks. In the most common form of multifactor authentication for a website, after you successfully enter your password, you are sent a six-digit PIN by text or email. You then enter the PIN on the website to complete authentication and gain access. If you have an option to activate multifactor authentication to protect your data on a website, you should seriously consider using it.

Smart Tip

Use multifactor authentication, if it is available. This is sometimes called two-step verification.

The term multifactor authentication means that more than one type of identification is used for authentication. One type of factor is something you know, like your password. Another type is something about you, like your fingerprints. A third type is something you have, such as your smartphone, used to receive a text or email, or a key fob that generates pseudorandom numbers. The numbers from the key fob are compared to numbers generated by the system you are logging into. A match verifies that you are in possession of the correct key fob.

Multifactor authentication is used to protect access to an ATM. You must insert a credit or debit card, which is something you have, then enter a four-digit PIN, something you know. The PIN is usually assigned by a bank, but it can be changed at your request.

Any personal information you share online, in an email, in a Facebook post, or in any other way can be used to steal your identity or to harm your family. Information that can be used to steal your identity includes your full name, your mother's maiden name, Social Security number (even just the last four digits), birthdate, address, driver's license number, phone number, and where you were born. Be careful when you share pictures or other information about your family, especially about children, even among people who are your friends. What makes you think this information will be limited only to these people once you share it online? Be careful when you "friend" people on Facebook and similar applications. Be sure you know anyone you accept as a friend to avoid sharing your friends-only personal information with hackers.

Smart Tip

Limit the amount of personal information you share online. Even if you want to share more, think twice about how your information might be misused and whether you need to share it.

You may think it's a bit extreme to not share even the last four digits of your Social Security number (SSN), but much of your full SSN can be determined from these four digits and just a little more information about you. Never give any part of your SSN to anyone or any organization that doesn't legitimately need it. If you are filling out a registration form in a doctor's office, try leaving the SSN entry blank. If they verbally request your SSN, ask why they really need it. Only provide the number after they give you convincing evidence that it is needed. Many medical practices no longer ask for it. The same goes for schools, including universities. Giving out your SSN can lead to identity theft, especially when combined with other personal information, such as your name and date of birth. How many people on Facebook know your date of birth? Have you considered changing the date by a few days so your friends can still celebrate your birthday while you avoid revealing sensitive information often used in identity theft?

Be careful when you post anything on an app like Facebook or a website about where you are traveling, if that information would let people know when you are not at home. You might as well post a sign that says, "Burglars, my home is all yours!" Don't tell people you don't know well when you

Smart Tip

Don't let people know when you are away from home.

are away from home or that you will be away from your home at a particular time. Remember this the next time you post a Facebook picture that shows you are on vacation.

Be very careful acting on any email you receive from someone you don't know or if the email looks the least bit suspicious. Look for misspellings or other discrepancies in emails. It's not safe to click on links in such emails or to click on attachments unless you have independently confirmed the source of the email by calling or texting the sender, not by responding

Smart Tip

Don't click on attachments to emails or web links in emails.

to the email. Be especially suspicious if the email asks you for sensitive personal information.

Cyberattackers are very good at spoofing emails from your friends and colleagues. Don't assume an email is safe even if it looks like it came from a friend or colleague. Alas, a friend may be innocently passing along a link to a website that has been corrupted by a cyberattacker. It is also possible that the friend's smartphone, PC, or email account may have been corrupted by a cyberattack, which may cause a dangerous email to be sent to you.

Be careful when you use a web browser to go to websites you are not familiar with and that may be dangerous, like porn sites. "Drive-by" cyber ambushes happen every day

Smart Tip

You should enter a web link directly into the web browser, character by character, rather than cutting and pasting the link from an email, even one from a person you know. Cutting and pasting can result in copying dangerous code that is not visible to you and that may contain malware. Once that code is entered into your browser, it can attack your system and your data.

Smart Tip

Be very careful about going to unfamiliar websites. Stay away from potentially dangerous websites, such as porn sites.

when people go to a website that has been compromised. Even reputable websites can get compromised, and the probability skyrockets with questionable websites. Many dangerous websites have URLs that look legitimate but may be off by a letter or a number.

Use caution when accessing banking and other financial websites using your PC, smartphone, or smart tablet. Be sure your device is as secure as possible, with firewall and antivirus protection on a PC (see later "Smart Tips") and by using smartphone or smart tablet apps that are supplied by or recommended by a bank or other financial institution. Never use a smartphone that has been "jailbroken"[79] to do financial tasks. These smartphones become vulnerable to many kinds of attacks and are not fully protected by the manufacturer-supported operating system. Be sure not to use a public Wi-Fi for financial applications, including Wi-Fi in hotel rooms, hotel business centers, and on airplanes.

Some websites for banking and other financial applications require that you answer "secret" questions for which you have previously entered the correct answer, such as the name of your best friend. Other sites, such as credit bureau websites, provide an even better level of multifactor authentication by asking questions only you are likely to be able to answer, such as addresses where you may have lived or worked years ago or your current mortgage payment.

Smart Tip

Be careful when you enter credit card or other financial information onto a website.

Be cautious when you enter credit card or other financial information onto a website. If you do so, such as to purchase something, make sure "https" is showing in front of the website's URL (usually shown on the top left of the page). This provides some assurance of the website's authenticity, and it adds security to your online conversation. Also, look for a padlock symbol, which provides additional assurance of the authenticity. It is not a good idea to leave your credit card information permanently on a shopping or travel site, since these kinds of websites have been compromised by cyberattacks in the past.

Avoid accessing sensitive personal information, including bank accounts, or entering credit card information, when using a public Wi-Fi or a public computer or kiosk, such as at a coffee shop, internet café, public library, airport, hotel, or on

Smart Tip

Consider using PayPal or ApplePay instead of credit cards to make payments for things you buy online. This reduces the number of times you have to "expose" your credit card information to websites and people and organizations you may not know.

an airplane. Beware that PCs in public places, such as hotel business centers, may not be running the latest software or have up-to-date antivirus protection. Cyberattackers may sometimes spoof Wi-Fi in public places, and all your online activities may be compromised! Don't assume that your hotel Wi-Fi is safe, whether you access it in your room or a business center accessible with your key card.

Key Word

A **jailbroken** smartphone is one that has been modified so it has unrestricted access to all underlying features of the phone, avoiding manufacturer restrictions limiting access only to approved apps. Some of the unapproved apps that can be loaded onto a jailbroken phone may contain malware that can lead to cyberattacks on the smartphone itself.

Smart Tip

Avoid accessing or entering sensitive personal information when using public Wi-Fi.

Generally, accessing the internet using your smartphone's cellular service rather than using public Wi-Fi is much safer, but not as safe as using a Virtual Private Network (VPN). Just turn the Wi-Fi off on your smartphone to make sure you are using your cell service. This has become more practical now that cell phone internet connectivity has become so fast in many places. I often get 25 Mbps or higher download speeds from my AT&T LTE cell phone service in many locations, almost as fast as on my home Wi-Fi. Be prepared for higher data usage on your cell phone bill if you do this.

Smart Tips

Use Virtual Private Network (VPN) software to encrypt data transmission when using your smartphone, smart tablet, or laptop computer in a public location, such as a coffee shop, airport, or hotel. Consider buying VPN software, since "free" VPNs, including those that come with your device, may not be as good as VPNs you can buy. Consult tech review sites to find current information on the best VPN software at a reasonable price.

Use cell service for web access rather than public Wi-Fi, if you prefer not to use a VPN.

When Using Your Smartphone

Smartphones that are unlocked can be used by anyone to do anything you can do with your smartphone, including reading email, posting on Facebook, and accessing sensitive personal information. Make sure your smartphone is set to lock automatically after a short time period and consider establishing a longer-than-minimum PIN (such as six digits rather than four) for unlocking your smartphone.

Keep your smartphone, smart tablet, and laptop in your possession. Don't leave them unattended in a public place, even for a minute. Don't use your smartphone to hold your place at a table in a restaurant while you get in line for service (yes, I have seen people do this, more than once). When you are in a crowded place with lots of people moving around, think twice about placing your smartphone on a table, even if you are sitting right next to it. It can disappear quickly when you are distracted.

Smart Tips

Make sure your smartphone is set to lock automatically. Also, activate the Find my iPhone or Find My Device (on an Android phone) app so you can find and manage your smartphone if it is lost or stolen.

If you are traveling, be careful about leaving mobile devices in a hotel room. Take them with you or secure them well when you leave the room, especially when you leave for meals or for meetings that have widely publicized schedules. Don't let someone else use your smartphone, even for a moment, unless they are family or a trusted friend.

In addition to avoiding public Wi-Fi when possible, you should avoid using public USB charging points or stations, such as in airports and on airplanes, or even those in hotel rooms.[80] The cord you use to charge your smartphone or other device can carry data and can be used to send harmful data to your phone without you being aware of it. Some of these public charging points have been compromised by cyberattackers, and as a result, can corrupt or destroy the content of your device. To be safe, you should not use such public USB charging points. Instead, use your own charger plugged into an electrical outlet, use a portable USB battery pack, or buy and use a USB charging cord that doesn't have the wires to transmit data.

Smart Tip

Don't use public USB charging points or stations.

Protect yourself and your smartphone by staying aware of your surroundings when you are away from home, especially when you are walking or running outside, while driving, or when sitting or standing in a public place. Turn the volume down on your earbuds so you can hear sounds around you. Don't set yourself up to be a victim of violence or an instant smartphone robbery when you are distracted while using your phone.

As hard as it may be for you to do it, never use your smartphone when you are crossing the street, even if you think the coast is clear. Pedestrians distracted while texting or talking on the phone have become victims of "snatch-and-run" cell phone thieves, while others have been hit by cars, resulting in injury and even death! Likewise, being distracted by texting or talking on the phone while driving has led to a significant increase in car accidents (see Chapter 3).

Check out apps for your smartphone and smart tablet before downloading and installing them. Attempt to verify that they are the "official" apps for banking and other important tasks rather than an imitation app that may be harboring

Smart Tip

Stay aware of your surroundings when walking, running, and driving, and when sitting or standing in a public place.

malware that can cause a cyberattack. Download the app from your bank's website or double-check that the name of the app on your bank's website is identical, to the letter, to the one you are about to load onto your smartphone.

Apps usually track your location by default. Look at the settings on your smartphone to see if location tracking is on for the app you have just loaded. Then determine whether the app really needs to know your location; if it doesn't, refuse to allow it access or change the location setting for that app on your smartphone. If an app has a legitimate reason for using location tracking, try to limit that access to when you are using each app rather than all the time. Delete any apps you no longer use. Because older apps may be updated to reduce cybersecurity vulnerabilities, you should keep your apps updated when new versions come out.

Smart Tip

Check out apps before installing them and delete them when they are no longer used.

Protection on the Homefront

All software on your PC and smartphone should be kept current with the latest security updates. This includes the operating system, web browser, and all applications software. Applications software includes word processing and spreadsheets, as well as add-on software such as Adobe Reader. Updates should be installed as soon as they are available, and your smartphone, PC, and other devices should be set for automatic updating if possible.

Smart Tip

Keep all software updated with the latest security patches. Set your PC, smartphone, and other devices for automatic updating.

Install antivirus/antimalware software that includes a firewall to help protect against cyberattacks. Be sure the virus definitions in the software are kept up to date by registering the software with the antivirus software developer. Don't forget to buy the new version of your antivirus software before your current subscription expires. This kind of software now protects against more than virus-type attacks, so it is sometimes called antimalware software.

Be sure to back up the contents of your smartphone, your smart tablet, and your PC—and do it often. Automatic backup to the cloud or to a hard drive makes this less of a chore. Consider backing up everything, including things like pictures and other data files, to both the cloud and to a hard drive.

Smart Tip

Install antivirus/antimalware software on your PC. Also, make sure your PC is set so the firewall in the operating system is turned on.

Backing up critical files to a flash drive (also called a thumb drive) that plugs into a USB port on your PC can help, too.

When using a web browser on your PC, smartphone, or smart tablet, heeding a few additional cybersecurity precautions is important. Web browsers have many software "plugins," which enable features such as Adobe Flash. Look for a link on your web browser to check and change the browser's settings. Some plugins can lead to vulnerabilities to cyberattacks. Although disabling Adobe Flash in browsers may reduce usability, cybersecurity experts sometimes recommend this step because Flash has become a widely known focal point for successful cyberattacks. At least make sure you are using the latest version of Adobe Flash and other

Key Word

A **firewall** is network security hardware and/or software that monitors incoming and outgoing network traffic and decides whether to allow or block specific traffic based on a defined set of security rules. A firewall can be implemented in hardware, software, or both.

browser plugins. From time to time, you should also consider clearing several kinds of data associated with your browser, such as saved passwords and your website visitation history.

Smart Tip

Your home Wi-Fi represents an opportunity for cyberattackers, but you can take a simple step to prevent this most of the time. Your home Wi-Fi router offers several encryption options. The best one is called WPA2 (which is short for Wi-Fi Protected Access 2). This setting uses the latest, strongest data encryption algorithm developed by the National Institute of Standards and Technology (NIST). You should select this option when setting up your router, which connects your house to the internet and to your PCs and other things. You should also enter a nondefault password so you have "administrative" access to and control of the router.

Key Word

A **default** username or password is built into devices, such as routers, when they are manufactured. Both the username and the password should be changed before using the device. This can be done in the settings during your device setup. Continuing to use a default password makes your device and every device connected to it vulnerable to cyberattack.

Smart Tip

Back up everything that you don't want to lose.

A "ransomware" attack occurs when a cyberattacker succeeds in taking over your PC, smart tablet, or smartphone, then demands a ransom payment before allowing you to regain access. The attacker "encrypts" the data and maybe the programs on your system and claims they will unencrypt your data after you have paid the ransom. You can take steps in advance to give yourself a fighting chance of recovering from such an attack.

To have a chance to recover without paying the ransom, it's a good idea to have more than one backup of everything on your system, perhaps located off-site so you can easily recover in case of theft, fire, or other disaster, in addition to a possible ransomware attack. Keep one or more backups of your data ei-

Smart Tip

Disable web browser plugins you may not need and that may make you vulnerable to cyberattack.

ther in the cloud or on an external hard drive you can plug into a USB port on your PC. If you leave your external hard drive connected to your PC, it is vulnerable to a ransom-type attack, just like the PC itself. Disconnect the external hard drive from the USB port when you're not backing up or restoring files. That way, if a cyberattacker takes over your PC, they won't be able hold your backup files for ransom. If you are the victim of this kind of attack, be sure to contact local law enforcement authorities before you do anything. They may be able to help you recover from the attack.

Smart Tip

Take steps in advance to be able to recover from a "ransomware" attack.

In the event of a ransom-type attack, be careful not to reconnect the external drive to your PC before the PC is purged of the malware that caused the attack. You may need to get some professional tech help to clean out your PC and to reload all the systems software and your data files.

Be very careful about thumb drives, also known as flash drives, that you receive for free at a convention or a store. It is best not to take them so you will not be tempted to use them or to use them by mistake. If you must use a thumb drive you have received under potentially suspicious conditions, run a virus scan on the device before using it. Some PCs and laptops are set up to do this automatically for you.

Prevent Identity Theft, Credit Card Fraud, and More

Watch for online and other news announcements of cybersecurity attacks that may have compromised your personal information. If you are notified that your sensitive personal information has likely been compromised, sign up for identity theft protection if it is offered as part of the notification. Then consider taking the minimum step to curtail access to your credit information, which is creating an "initial fraud alert" at one of the three credit bureaus. That credit bureau will notify the other two bureaus. This alert will ensure that lenders and other people who check your credit know that you are potentially the victim of identity theft. As a result, they may take extra steps to verify your identity, such as contacting you personally. You may also want to sign up for an initial fraud alert if you have lost your wallet or Social Security card, or if other personal, financial, or account information is lost or stolen. An initial fraud alert is good for a year, and you can request another alert the day after it expires. If you are the victim of identity theft, you can request an "extended fraud alert," which lasts for seven years in most states.[81]

Smart Tip

Don't use a thumb drive you received for free at a convention or a store. Don't plug it into anything!

If you want to take more serious action, you can request a "credit freeze" by contacting all three credit bureaus. No one inquiring about your credit will be able to access your credit file until you remove the freeze. While your credit is frozen, you cannot establish new credit, including obtaining a new credit card. A credit freeze is supposed to last forever, unless you remove it. Unfreezing your credit file can be done in an hour or

Smart Tip

Stay alert for news or information about cyberattacks, especially if you believe you may have been compromised. Also watch out for email alerts and notices in the mail that may say that you have been potentially compromised. Activate a credit fraud alert or credit freeze if you want increased protection against fraud.

so online or by phone, or it may take a few days by mail, and you will have to ask each credit bureau to do so. If you unfreeze your credit at one or more of the credit bureaus, you will have to re-establish the freeze to continue this protection.

It is scary to receive a notification that your personal information may have been stolen or otherwise exposed. Most of the time, the organization notifying you does not know for sure that your personal information was compromised, but they are taking the precaution of notifying you, just in case. Sometimes, you may see charges on one or more of your credit cards that you didn't make. This may just mean the credit card's information has been stolen and used fraudulently, and all you have to do is notify the credit card issuer. If debit card information is stolen and used fraudulently, you may not be so lucky. US law requires that credit card issuers hold you liable for a maximum of $50 in this situation, and most issuers will make sure you suffer no loss. But if debit card information is misused, you may lose all the money in the bank account it is associated with, and you may not get any of it back. Some banks may be willing to work with you in this kind of situation, so be sure to ask.

It gets more serious, however, if you find out that your

address has been changed on a bank account or a credit card, or that your bank account has been drained. New credit cards may have also been issued in your name with a different address, and bills may have been run up on them. It anything like this happens to you, you need to notify the credit card issuer, your bank, and a credit bureau; then seek professional advice about how to regain control of your identity. It may be helpful to report identity theft to the FTC on its IdentityTheft.gov website.

Watch your bank statements when you receive them in the mail or, preferably, more frequently online, to make sure

Key Words

Credit card fraud is when someone steals your credit card information and runs up unauthorized charges on your credit card account. **Identity theft** is when someone gets enough information about you to "steal" your identity. If they have your SSN and your name, date of birth, and maybe a little more information about you, they may be able to establish new bank accounts and credit cards in your name. They may also be able to take over your existing bank accounts and credit cards, even changing the name, mailing address, and email address on these accounts. You may not find out that you have become the victim of identity theft until long after you have lost lots of money and find yourself unable to establish new accounts or to close accounts that have been taken over.

How to Reach the Credit Bureaus

The FTC has provided contact information for each of the three major credit bureaus: Equifax, Experian, and TransUnion.[217]

- Equifax
  Equifax.com/personal/credit-report-services
  (800) 685-1111
- Experian
  Experian.com/help
  888-EXPERIAN (888-397-3742)
- TransUnion
  TransUnion.com/credit-help
  (888) 909-8872

you catch any unauthorized charges. It pays to take a few precautions to avoid credit card fraud or, even worse, identity theft. You should also review your credit card statements when you receive them or more frequently online to make sure no unauthorized charges have appeared.

Watch out for emails or telephone calls from unknown persons who say your personal information has been compromised. Never trust Caller ID to identify the person calling. Information about incoming callers and calling numbers can be spoofed by crooks. Don't click on any link or attached file in an email, and independently check out the possibility of compromise by going to a known website or checking the current news. Never give permission to someone whose email you have received or who has called you on the phone offering to remove malware on your PC or smartphone or to fix it for you, and don't even think about giving them a credit card number to pay for their "help." This kind of ploy often results in your credit card information and the data on your PC or smartphone

Smart Tip

Don't get scammed by emails or telephone callers who say your personal information has been compromised.

being stolen. Your PC or smartphone may also be harmed, too, by having data and even programs deleted or changed.

When using an ATM, you should exercise special precautions, because thieves often watch people enter their PINs, either in person or with a camera or other device they have attached to the machine. ATMs located in convenience or grocery stores and other nonbank locations are especially vulnerable. When possible, use an ATM at a bank and in a neighborhood that doesn't look too rough. Use the ATM during the day, not at night, and during the week when the machines are monitored more closely by the banks. Use an ATM inside the bank if one is available. Look very closely at the ATM itself for things that don't look right, such as an overlay around the card-entry slot that may be a "skimmer," which can steal your card information, or a camera aimed at the key pad (such as a camera behind a small "pinhole" in the ATM housing, which could be very hard to see), which can be used to steal your PIN. *Be sure to use one hand to shield the hand that is entering the PIN just in case there is a camera nearby or someone is watching.*[82] If anything looks loose on the ATM or doesn't look like it usually does, run for the hills and find another ATM.

Also, be on the lookout for individuals standing around or sitting in nearby cars who may be able to watch you enter your PIN, or who may even identify you as a potential candidate for a robbery after you take cash out of the ATM. These types of criminals have been known to watch a person walking away or getting into their car, then following them, stopping them, and robbing them or worse.

You should also look carefully at credit card readers on gasoline pumps, the ones at grocery store checkout lanes, and at sales counters in retail stores to make sure there are no obvious signs of tampering. Try to use gas pumps that have key locks on their doors, especially little access doors near the credit card reader. Also, look for security cameras aimed at the pumps and possibly for official-looking sealing tape across access doors. Choose pumps that are near the gas station where the attendant can see them, not way out near the street. It may be safer to pay inside rather than at the pump.

Smart Tip

Take precautions when using an ATM to protect yourself, your PIN, and your money.

Be careful when using credit card readers at self-checkout lanes in stores because they may not be monitored closely by store personnel. If you don't like the looks of a credit card reader, take the time to go through an attended lane with a cashier. And look carefully at the credit card reader in that lane, too. One type of credit-card skimmer looks just like a real card reader, but it sits on top of the real card reader and steals your information. Look for anything out of the ordinary, including anything loose. All it takes is a few seconds for someone to attach a skimmer, and it may be hard to spot!

You are better protected from fraud when you use your

credit card with a chip, although it is possible to be compromised when using a chip card, too.[83] You should be careful when you give your credit or debit card to a server in a restaurant or to a clerk in a retail store who takes it away from you to enter it into the store's transaction entry system, which, unfortunately, is the norm in the US. Be especially suspicious if there is a delay returning the card to you! It only takes a few seconds to skim or copy the information from your card, from the magnetic stripe on your card, or from the visible information on it, which can then be used to make unauthorized charges to your card. If your card isn't returned reasonably soon, ask somebody about it, but don't make a scene. Everything is likely OK, but it pays to be cautious.

Smart Tip

Look carefully for anything suspicious before using credit card readers on gasoline pumps and in retail stores.

Now that most of us have chip cards, we are a little safer from this kind of attack. But we are not as safe as people are in Europe, where the server or clerk usually brings a mobile credit card reader to the customer and either lets us insert the card or performs the transaction in front of us, while we watch carefully.

Be especially wary about handing over your debit card because, as I stated earlier, debit card issuers are not required by law to help you with fraudulent transactions. With a credit card, you are limited to a maximum of $50 potential loss.

In this chapter, we have learned that it takes a team to protect our systems and data from cyberattacks. That team includes software developers who issue security updates, or patches, to their software, as well as the developers of the antivirus software that we buy and load on our PCs and sometimes our smartphones. These team members are especially helpful when they send automatic updates with the latest virus protection. Online store owners, brick-and-mortar retailers, restaurants, and banks contribute to the team by making sure adequate cyber protection is provided on their systems, which reduces our risk when we shop using credit cards. *You, too, are an important member of the team.* Protect yourself by watching out for unusual activity online, using long and complex passwords, setting Wi-Fi parameters to protect systems and data, and practicing all the other steps you've learned about in this chapter.

It's not easy to be part of this team! It sometimes takes the time and energy we'd rather apply to other activities, such as working or spending time with family and friends. But if you do your part, take the need for cyber protection seriously, and follow the tips in this chapter, you will be able to enjoy your high-tech devices more and worry less about cyberattacks. You don't have to do everything I have recommended. I have listed the "Smart Tips" in each category in priority order. But the more you do, the more likely you will be able to enjoy new technology without being the victim of a cyberattack or identity theft.

In the next chapter, we step back in time to explore the history of technology so we can learn why it has evolved to what we have today, which will help us understand it better. By exploring the historical background of the high-tech gadgets we know and love, you will be in a better position to take advantage of today's technology—and tomorrow's.

Cybersecurity for Kids

Parents and educators should be extra vigilant when it comes to online safety for children because the threats may be greater for them and they are not old enough to understand those threats. Here are some special cybersecurity tips for parents and educators to help keep kids safe. These tips are taken from online publications of the US Department of Homeland Security:[218]

- Start conversations regularly with younger children about practicing online safety.
- When very young children start using a computer, they should be supervised closely by a parent or caregiver.
- Explain to your kids why it is a good idea to only post information they are comfortable with others seeing.
- Kids should know that they shouldn't talk with strangers online and that they should never agree to meet someone in person who they do not already know well.
- Help children understand that personal information should be kept private. They should avoid sharing their name, address, phone number, birthday, passwords, and the name of their school when online.

Key Points

- Our PCs, smartphones, and other systems are often vulnerable to cyberattacks due to errors in the software that have not yet been corrected through updates known as software patches.
- Cyberattacks range from intrusions by hackers who are using attack software downloaded from the internet to the advanced cyberattacks using sophisticated, new attack tools.
- We can do things to help protect our systems and our data, including our sensitive personal information. It only takes a small number of precautions to provide significant protection.
- When online, use long, complex passwords and different passwords for each website or account. Also, use multifactor authentication if it is available. Don't click on links or attachments in emails from people you don't know.
- When using your smartphone, set it to lock automatically after a short period of time and don't use public Wi-Fi unless you have a VPN installed.
- On your PC at home and on your smartphone, keep all software updated with the latest software patches. Setting these kinds of devices to update automatically works best. Install antivirus/antimalware protection on your home PC, and make sure it is continually updated.
- Back up all your data often, to the cloud or to an external disk drive.

CHAPTER 5

TECHNOLOGY — A HISTORICAL PERSPECTIVE

YOU WILL BE ABLE to understand new technology better if we look at how technology came of age and how it became so important in our lives. The technology we depend on today builds on older technology developed over many years. Historically, technology evolved based on people's needs and wants, coupled with what scientists and engineers invented and were able to apply in a practical way. By exploring how perceived needs contributed to new technology in the past, we can develop a better appreciation for how the technology we have now relates to our needs.

New high-tech devices must meet our needs to be successful, even if we didn't realize we had some of those needs until we had a smartphone in our hand or access to much of the world's information through the web. Sometimes, new technology suddenly appears and we wonder how we ever lived without it. Other times, new technology is so intriguing that it can appear to be magical or mysterious — even miraculous. It reminds me of this quote from Albert Einstein: *There are only two ways to live your life. One is as though nothing is a miracle. The other is as though everything is a miracle.*

In this chapter, we will start at the beginning, with the primitive tools that humans developed to help cope with the

Key Word

Historically, the word **technology** has carried different meanings over time. When applied to early human history, the term focused on tool use. One useful definition of technology is "tools and machines that may be used to solve real-world problems."[219] Another definition focuses on "the practical application of knowledge."[220]

world around them. These tools helped the early prehumans and humans to hunt and eat, build shelter, and stand up for themselves when threatened. Then we will quickly transition to modern times, when engineers and scientists developed sophisticated tools to help meet many of our higher-level needs, like tools to help us calculate, analyze, and manipulate data, and convert data to meaningful information.

Computers, and things that contain computers, are so much a part of our lives today that we often think of them first when we think of technology, even though we rely on many other types of technology every day. We will follow the

For the Tech Curious

Some new developments build on past advances in a systematic way, such as the forward march of computers, with smaller, higher-performance components following an architecture that has been around for decades. Other developments are more revolutionary, such as the internet, social networking, and smartphones. Revolutionary developments tend to be more disruptive to our lives, for better or worse.

evolution of computers starting with early, giant mainframes and progressing to our current world of PCs, smartphones, and computers in the cloud. We will explore efforts by pioneers to make computers user-friendly, which inspired things like the web and smart speakers that use artificial intelligence to help them respond to our requests.

Going Way Back in Time

Technological development has been motivated for centuries by basic survival and perceived warfare needs, as well as higher-level economic and life needs. Technology enables us to do more, enjoy a more meaningful life, and connect with each other better. Early stone tools that date back 3 million years, developed by the predecessors of humans as we know them, could be considered the first technology.[84] They used these tools to cut and prepare new foods, including meat from large animals. A few million years later, humans learned to make pottery. The invention of the plow allowed for new methods of growing food, and, about 4,000 years ago, the wheel was invented. By the end of the 10th century AD, inventions included cast iron, the catapult, glass, and watermills, as well as the concept of zero as a number, gunpowder, and toilet paper.[85] During the next six centuries, things moved faster. Mechanical clocks were created, along with the spinning wheel, movable type and the printing press, and the first mechanical calculator, built in 1642 by Blaise Pascal.

Moving ahead to the 1700s, the Industrial Revolution was the transition to new manufacturing processes. New developments in textile manufacturing, mining, metallurgy, and transport were driven by the steam engine. In the 1800s came the first steam locomotive, refrigeration, the telephone, the first practical light bulb, and what could be called the first general purpose computer, the Babbage Analytical Engine, conceived by Charles Babbage in 1834.[86]

A lot of the technology we think has been around forever was not invented until the 20th century.[87] The Wright brothers flew in 1903. Movies with sound, penicillin, the jet engine, radar, and television were invented in the 1920s and 1930s. The first nuclear reactor and the transistor were invented in the 1940s. Velcro and car seat belts were invented in the 1950s and Touch-Tone (push button) telephones in 1963.

The Dawn of the Computer Age

In 1944, Howard Aiken built the Harvard Mark I and Mark II, for which programs were placed on punched paper tape that was fed into the computers using paper-tape readers. These computers were constructed from mechanical relays. A key person who designed the programs was the famous Grace Hopper, a computer pioneer, educator, programmer, and programming languages expert. Her team discovered a moth stuck between the contacts on one of the many mechanical relays inside the Mark II computer, and it became famous as the first computer "bug"![88] A copy of a page of the log book for this computer dated September 9, 1947, shows the moth, under transparent tape, and an annotation "First actual case of bug being found."[89]

The ENIAC (Electronic Numerical Integrator and Computer) was completed in 1945 at the Moore School of the University of Pennsylvania. It was used to improve the US Army's ability to calculate artillery firing tables. ENIAC was an electronic computer programmed with plug boards and cables, not with an internal stored-program memory.[90] Another early design for a computer was developed by John Atanasoff in 1939. This design would have resulted in the world's first electronic digital computer, but only a prototype was ever built.[91]

A prototype of an electronic stored-program computer, the SSEM (Small Scale Experimental Machine), was placed into "hesitant operation" in the UK, at Manchester University, in

1948, according to the British Computer Society.[92] And a fully functional electronic stored-program computer, the EDSAC (Electronic Delay Storage Automatic Calculator), was built at Cambridge University in 1949.

The National Bureau of Standards (NBS) SEAC (Standards Eastern Automatic Computer), the first electronic stored-program computer built in the US, was placed into operation in 1950.[93] A year later, under the technical oversight of Sam Alexander, who had led the SEAC design team, the first UNIVAC I was completed by the Remington Rand Corporation and installed at the US Census Bureau.[94] Computer development continued at NBS (now known as NIST, the National Institute of Standards and Technology) for a couple of decades.

Early computers were BIG! They occupied a whole room, sometimes even more than a room. I experienced the thrill of walking inside the NBS SEAC computer, being very careful not to touch anything, because in those days there was high voltage everywhere inside the computer to power the vacuum tubes. We were able to touch the outside of big computers in the early days, to flip switches on the front of the computer or on a control panel. We were also able to get an idea of what was going on inside by looking at flashing lights on the front of these computers that "looked cool" and generally displayed useful information about the status of the computer and the program it was running.

Computer programs were run one at a time, and they were entered into the computer on punched cards or punched paper tape. To load a program into a computer, then run or "execute" it, a "boot sequence" was set up using switches on the front of the computer. This is what I did as a freshman at Carnegie Institute of Technology in 1960, when I took a computer science course that required students to write programs for an IBM 650 computer. We typed the programs using a key-punch machine, which punched holes that represented the program in a "deck" of punched cards. Then we entered the card deck into a punched-card reader and flipped switches on the computer to start the boot sequence while looking at the lights on the control panel to guide us. Once the program on the card deck had been entered into the computer, it would be executed, resulting in a printout of the program, the data generated by the program, and error messages. In a sense, this large computer was our personal computer, since it belonged to just one of us at a time and we were up close and personal with it.

Computers Behind Glass

However, after a while, users were separated from the large computers, which were placed behind glass walls to protect them and help keep them cool. Users were no longer allowed to touch them, so they sent their punched card decks to computer operators, who served the card decks to the computers and delivered the resulting printouts to us. This kept the expensive computers working efficiently while the users waited and waited for the results.

We never gave up wanting to be physically close to our new technology, including touching the computer when possible. Some of the very early computers had electric typewriter-like devices known as Flexowriters or teletypewriters that enabled us to type into the computers, which would type back to us. Dartmouth College in New Hampshire hosted an early demonstration of remote access to a computer using a teletypewriter that communicated over a telephone line with a computer at Bell Laboratories in New Jersey.[95]

Time-shared computing systems were invented in the interest of connecting people to their computers in a more effective way. Because computers performed their computations many times faster than people, time-sharing enabled several people to use a computer at the same time. Each person interacted with the computer directly, through a teletypewriter terminal, and felt they had a computer all to themselves. But there was only one computer, and it was somewhere else, in another room or maybe in a distant city. This apparently simultaneous access to what seemed like our very own computer was an illusion resulting from the speed mismatch between the relatively slow human users and the fast computer. I wrote the operating system software at NBS for an early research time-sharing system in 1967. I also wrote a chapter on time-shared computers that was published in the book *Advances in Computers, Volume 8.*[96] Time-sharing helped users feel "closer" to the computers, even though they were generally far away from it. You could say that it felt almost like having your own PC.

The Rise of the Personal Computer

Even with time-sharing, the computer was still kept isolated, often behind glass walls in an air-conditioned room. Then the world changed. Personal computers (PCs) were born! Beginning as a fun pastime by the hobbyist community, some folks began to make their own computers. The technology of the day, including transistors and integrated circuits, made it possible for these computers to sit on or under a table in front of a user rather than somewhere else. The first publicly available PC was the Altair, which was introduced in 1975 and came as a do-it-yourself kit.[97] Once assembled, it was programmed by moving switches and watching lights on its front panel. Bill Gates and Paul Allen, the co-founders of Microsoft, designed their first software for the Altair, which enabled it to execute programs written in the emerging BASIC programming language. This software, an "interpreter," translated each BASIC command into the language of the computer (machine language). BASIC was intended to make it much easier to program a computer than in the past.

Then came Steve Wozniak, who designed the Apple I computer in 1976.[98] Steve Jobs helped him with marketing, which was focused largely on do-it-yourself "homebrew" computer hobbyists. It wasn't a complete computer, since you had to attach a keyboard and use a TV monitor as the display. When Wozniak designed the Apple II, with his friend and colleague Jobs in a lead marketing role, it was still not much more than a hobbyist effort, until Dan Bricklin built software for the Apple II that enabled people to build and use spreadsheets. This software was called VisiCalc. I remember how exciting it was to use VisiCalc. In fact, I bought an Apple II for work to be able to perform project management financial calculations using this automated spreadsheet. The first widely known and used personal computer, the IBM PC, was introduced in 1981, and the Apple Macintosh followed in 1984.

Speaking of PCs and related technology, some of the most fascinating and influential work on this type of technology was done at the Xerox Palo Alto Research Center (PARC).[99] I had a chance to sit around on bean bags with some of my colleagues at PARC in the 1970s to discuss the incredible things being developed there and where new technology was headed. The technology created at PARC included the Alto workstation (the first real personal computer), with bit-mapped graphical user interface technology and a mouse that enabled a user to use windowed displays, symbols (called icons), and menus, instead of typing commands. The Alto included the Bravo editor, which looked a lot like Word and was "what you see is what you get," (WYSIWYG). It was connected to a Dover laser printer through the Ethernet, a new type of local network that interconnected workstations, printers, and other local devices to each other and, eventually, to networks like the internet.

The Ethernet was invented by Bob Metcalfe and his colleagues at PARC. It became the dominant local networking technology in the world and has enjoyed widespread use for years for local networking in homes, offices, and industrial applications. It has even been used as one of the interconnection networks within some supercomputers and as the high-speed network connection capability that ties together various parts of the internet.[100] Bob Metcalfe also created "Metcalfe's Law," which says the effect or value of a network is proportional to the square of the number of connected users or devices. Or, the more participants in the network, the more valuable the network is to everyone! This concept applies to the internet, social networking websites, and lots of other things.[101]

We all depend on this technology today in our homes and offices, which gives us the capability to create and modify digital documents containing text and graphics, store them, print them, and share them. It is the technology that Apple's Mac

Key Word

WYSIWYG (what you see is what you get; pronounced "wizzy-wig") means that as you create a document using a text editor, possibly including pictures and other images, you see an image just like the finished product will appear when printed or sent to someone else. This development made computer printed and displayed output "come alive," rather than look old fashioned and overwhelming, usually using only one hard-to-read type font and no graphics.

and Microsoft's Windows were based on. In 1977, I led an effort to bring this technology—Alto computers with the Bravo editor and Dover printers and the Ethernet—to Washington as part of our work at NBS to identify and test new technology for future federal government operational use. We installed it at the White House, the House of Representatives, the Senate, and NBS. The technology was found to be very promising but not yet mature enough for routine use.

Networking Comes of Age

Another key technology we have become very dependent on is computer networking. In the early days of computing, typewriter-like computer terminals were connected by wires or cables directly to a computer. Then, remote connections were made using dial-up or dedicated telephone lines, at very slow data rates. Some computers were connected to other computers using telephone lines. Starting in the 1980s, many people gained access to online services like AOL, Genie, Prodigy, and CompuServe over telephone lines, using dial-up access.[102] Users of these online services were able to access email, news, games, and other capabilities. By 1993, AOL began providing access to the internet for its users.

In the 1960s, research led to the use of telephone lines to send data at higher speeds. New approaches were developed for sharing telephone lines and improving the efficiency of data transmission. One approach for sharing and routing data to different computers was called "packet switching." Data was sent a small amount at a time, in what was called a packet, along with information about where the packet should be sent. This contrasted with "circuit switching," which was the technology that telephone systems were built on, but that was not very efficient for transmitting data.

One of the earliest packet-switching networks was called

the ARPANET (or Advanced Research Projects Agency Network).[103] The ARPANET was a predecessor of the internet, and it began operation in 1969. I had firsthand experience with the ARPANET as part of a research program I led at NBS. We had a Terminal Interface Message Processor (TIP) node of the ARPANET to support research, especially in partnership with ARPA academic researchers.[104] Development of the ARPANET was motivated by a US Department of Defense need for more robust and reliable military communications. In the late 1980s, the internet grew out of the ARPANET and other government-sponsored efforts, such as the NSFNET, which was funded by the National Science Foundation. The backbones of these networks used telephone company-provided communication lines and modems, initially operating at 56

Key Words

A **node** of the ARPANET was a computer that functioned as a router, connecting one or more computers to the ARPANET through long-distance communications lines to other ARPANET routers. Each router was programmed to decide where each packet of data should go next on its way to its destination. Most of these ARPANET routers were called **IMPs (Interface Message Processors)**. A **TIP (Terminal Interface Message Processor)** was an IMP that also had an interface for terminals, like teletypewriters and display terminals, to connect them to the internet without going through a separate computer connected to the IMP.

Kilobits per second (Kbps) and then at T1 speed, 1.5 Megabits per second (Mbps), which was high speed at the time but very slow by current standards. Users connected to these networks by accessing their local research computers, which were, in turn connected to the ARPANET or the NSFNET.

As the internet began operation, individual users connected to it by dialing the phone number of a network access point. They communicated through telephone lines, at a speed up to about 14 Kbps, extraordinarily slow by today's standards. Then, cable TV operators and other companies began providing higher-speed user access to the internet at speeds that are now up to hundreds of megabits per second and even faster. These companies became known as internet service providers (ISPs). The ISPs also operate some of the "backbone" high-speed communications links of the internet.

The World Wide Web, which many of us think of when we hear the term internet, was first envisioned in 1989 by Tim Berners-Lee and came into general use in about 1994.[105] The web is one widely used application on the internet that enables users to access multimedia information. This information is in the form of a webpage that contain images, text, and data. We can access data files and real-time video on the web, as well as perform transactions on interactive shopping, financial, and other websites.[106] The internet existed well before the web, but it was difficult to use and not particularly friendly. It became accessible to the masses in 1995, when several companies began providing low-speed dial-up access to the internet and when off-the-shelf web browsers became available.[107] Most of the early websites contained information in graphical and text form that could be viewed and downloaded by internet users. The introduction of search services like Google made this information more accessible.

In a Server Farm Far, Far Away

Networking has helped move technology to new forms of computing in which computers on our desktops and in our smartphones work together with larger computers elsewhere. Our "big" computers are behind the walls again, physically separated from their users, but now the big computers are networks of smaller computers that are called "server" computers. Most of these server computers are in giant data centers that each hold many thousands of server computers in what are called "server farms." They are not behind glass walls anymore. They are in fortress-like buildings with high security.

Using smartphones, smart tablets, and PCs, we connect through the internet to the server farms, which can be far away. We don't know where they are, and they can be anywhere in our country or even in another country on another continent. There are hundreds of large data centers that house the server computers that make Google, Facebook, Amazon, and other websites possible. These large data centers, which we never see or touch in person, are at the forefront of computing and networking technology today. All this technology is complex and, as a result, somewhat fragile, even though millions of people and businesses rely on it every day.

In the aggregate, these large data centers are what we refer to when we talk about the "cloud." The cloud incorporates "virtualized" computing capabilities, and we don't know or care which physical server computer is supporting us. We don't need to know. Computing in a data center is configured for high reliability, with backup equipment for computing and storage, along with redundant communications capability, multiple sources of electric power, and uninterruptible power systems that use generators and batteries. Redundancy frequently involves other data centers that can even be in different countries, configured to back up each other. If a user needs much more computational capability than usual, it's there to be tapped. If a user wants to store a large database, the storage capacity is also ready and waiting.

We have grown accustomed to being connected to the cloud through our smartphones, smart tablets, and PCs that are tied through the internet to what seems like an almost infinite amount of computational capability and data storage. As a result, our ability to interact with our clever, computer-enabled technological assistants is far better than in the early days of computing because the mobile devices themselves are more capable and are connected to even more capability in the cloud. The user interface for these devices is much easier to use, too. In the early days, it was like speaking Greek to our computers. Computer users were almost always programmers, because you had to know esoteric programming languages and machine language (what the computer hardware understands) to "talk" to your computer. It was "do it yourself" computing.

Key Word

A **user interface** is the means through which a user and a device communicate. It can include a keyboard and a display and display formats that are easy to comprehend, as well as user commands that are easy to use.

Making Computers User Friendly

One of the early leaders setting the stage for truly usable computers was J. C. R. Licklider, a professor at MIT and a leader of ARPA, the US Department of Defense agency that developed the ARPANET. "Lick," as he was known, was inspiring as a psychologist-turned-computer scientist, who became a leader of the entire computing and networking community. His 1960 paper "Man-Computer Symbiosis,"[108] gave hope that, someday, humans and computers could work together to accomplish great things.

Another early leader developing the concepts critical to today's technology was Vannever Bush, who envisioned what he called Memex.[109] The Memex concept was a personal information system in which an individual could peruse text and make "associations," or links, between that text and other text. These associations were intended to make connections between information, similar to how the brain works. Bush's work inspired Ted Nelson, Doug Engelbart, Andy van Dam, and others to envision the use of "hyperlinks" that connect to content elsewhere that is related to what we are reading.[110] Does this sound familiar? All this contributed to Tim Berners-Lee's work at a European research facility in Switzerland, called CERN, to create the World Wide Web.[111] It also inspired Marc Andreessen, then at the University of Illinois, and his team to create Mosaic in 1993, the first widely used web browser incorporating text and graphics.[112]

Great minds were following other great minds in this process, and Andreessen even included a "collaboration" capability in an early version of Mosaic similar to a feature of Memex. This Mosaic function allowed users to download a document, work on it, and repost it.[113] If Andreessen had found a practical way to make this work, a significant part of Bush's Memex dream would have been implemented, and perhaps be in general use today, but this Mosaic function did not survive beyond early versions of the browser.

With his Memex concept, Bush envisioned people searching for and viewing a page of information (on microfilm in those days), which they could connect to another page in the same or another document. These links represented one person's path through the pages of information. The path was documented so another person could follow the first person's trail and learn from it, while another person might be taking a different path from page to page. With lots of people viewing pages and creating links, there would soon be some organization among the pages that made sense. In addition, people would also know the sequence of the pages.

The web uses links across pages, between one word or picture and another, just like Memex. In addition to the web, other new tools for creating links among pages have been proposed, but, overall, we are still overwhelmed by all the information we face every day, as we try to organize and make sense of it without help from others who have read the same information.

For the most part, as we are reading and following links on the web we are making our way through a great array of information and knowledge but not actually creating new knowledge as we do so. Tim Berners-Lee, the inventor of the World Wide Web, is reported to have criticized the Mosaic browser, the first practical web browser, for being just a web publishing platform, rather than including a collaborative capability like Memex.[114] To this day, web browsers enable us to look at web-published content but do not enable us to work together with others who are browsing the web. One exception to this is the online collaborative encyclopedia Wikipedia, through which thousands of individuals participate in creating and updating content that millions of people rely on every day. Wikipedia provides a capability that goes part way toward the Memex concept by enabling individuals to read, edit, and add content to a large amount of accessible information.

Technology in Our Lives

Our historical tour of technology has led to a world where we are surrounded by technology. It is our constant companion when we are at home or the office, whether we are driving or riding public transportation, while we are walking down the street or lounging at the beach. Many of us carry or wear technology wherever we go, which could be in the form of a smartphone, smart tablet, Apple Watch, or fitness band. And that just scratches the surface of the technology that surrounds us.

At home, we probably have technology in every room. HDTVs are most likely in more than one room, and higher-resolution, higher-quality TV is already on the way. Devices like Roku, Amazon FireTV, Google Chromecast, and Apple TV connect to video-streaming sources like Netflix, Amazon, and YouTube through the internet.[115] TVs have become smarter, and can include computers, cameras, and microphones, for better and for worse. Check out the discussion of "Always Watching, Always Listening" in Chapter 3.

New types of devices help automate homes, with devices like the Nest thermostat that can automatically set the heating and air conditioning in the "best way" to keep us comfortable after sensing household occupancy and learning our temperature preferences. The Ecobee (sometimes shown with a number after it, like 3 or 4, to denote these models) thermostat performs similar functions and makes homes more comfortable by using temperature and occupancy sensors in multiple rooms. It can provide "finer" temperature control, down to 0.5 degrees. Of course, finer temperature control means that the heat or cooling goes on and off more often, introducing a little additional wear and tear on the system. The Ecobee and the Nest work with Amazon Alexa. The Ecobee also works with Apple HomeKit, which is a framework for Apple products to control what Apple calls "connected accessories" in the home, such as lights, locks, and thermostats so we can do things like telling Siri to turn down the temperature. The Nest thermostat can now be connected to clothes washers and dryers and other things. And through the "Works with Nest" program, it can use sensor information about whether families are home or away to coordinate home energy use.[116]

Nest and Ecobee can both perform their basic temperature-control tasks without a connection to the internet. But with Wi-Fi and internet access, they can both be controlled by a smartphone, smart tablet, or PC from anywhere. With both thermostats, the homeowner is dependent on the continued reliable operation of the manufacturer's website for advanced control and support features, including downloading updated thermostat software.

One fascinating type of new device that has gained popularity is the smart speaker, which listens for voice commands and can play music, respond to questions, and control things around the house. Some smart speakers sit on tabletops. Others are embedded in devices like smart thermostats and smart wall switches. The Amazon Echo devices are home to "Alexa," which listens for someone to say "Alexa," then listens for voice questions or commands. It is connected through Wi-Fi and the internet to the Amazon cloud so it can perform these functions. Google Home is another smart speaker that performs similar functions. Apple iPhones, iMacs, Apple Watches, Apple TVs, and Apple HomePod have Siri, who listens for our questions and commands and responds verbally. Siri can initiate actions, such as setting reminders and dimming the lights in the home.

It wasn't that long ago that home felt safe from the intrusions of programmable things, devices that go beep in the night and might need to be rebooted because they have lost their way. Now, almost every room has at least something with programmable logic, and most of us carry around our own computers in our smartphones, smart tablets, and other mobile devices. This is all part of the Internet of Things. Be sure to read Chapter 8, "The Things Are Coming!"

We are increasingly comfortable with everyday things around the home that don't look like or behave like computers but contain embedded computers or at least programmable logic that "gives them a mind of their own." When these things do something unusual or just "lock up," we have become accustomed to unplugging them, waiting several seconds, and plugging them back in. With any luck, they will work like new again after this rebooting process. Some of these devices have a reset button, which makes rebooting easier.

When We Think of New Technology, We Think of Computers

It is no wonder that we think of computers and all things digital when we think of new technology. We picture new digital electronic gadgets, such as smartphones, smart tablets, PCs, smart TVs, home automation devices, smart cars, and the internet.

We accept that computers and computer-based devices are a part of our lives every day. Embedded computers have for some years been an effective way to build control logic into smart things. These smart things have memory to store programs and the data that enables the things to work. The programs may be stored in flash, or similar nonvolatile memory, in which case they are referred to as firmware. Nonvolatile memory retains its content even if it loses power. The firmware can usually be updated to add functionality or to fix bugs. The programs for the Nest and Ecobee thermostats are stored in firmware, and these programs are regularly updated through the internet. Chapter 8, "The Things Are Coming," includes a discussion of some of the vulnerabilities of devices that cannot be updated this way, leading to potential cyberattacks.

Many lessons can be learned from the development of new technologies of all types since the dawn of humankind. We first need to be aware of the impact that new technologies have had over the years on people in general and ourselves personally, as well as on our communities and culture. We should be aware of the ways high-tech gadgets are improving our lives, but also how they may be negatively impacting us. When we get resentful of the care and feeding our devices take, we need to look at ourselves relative to people just a few decades ago who had much less technology to help them and thus had less time to enjoy their lives. Yet we cannot forget to look toward the future as well and consider how tech will fit into our lives (which is addressed in Chapter 10, "What's in our Future").

Next, we will examine a running theme from the early chapters, which deserves its own spotlight because of its importance in our lives: "complexity."

Key Points

- You will be able to understand new technology better if you look at how technology came of age and how it became so important in our lives.
- The history of technology began with stone-age tools and progressed over thousands of years to pottery and the wheel, then to the printing press and the light bulb, and finally to computers.

- Early computers were very large and were kept behind glass in temperature-controlled rooms. Users sometimes ran everything, pushing buttons on the computers and entering their software programs themselves. Advancing technology and lower-cost hardware made the idea of a personal computer possible. Researchers also developed ways to make computers easier to use, with text editors and spreadsheet software. The idea was to have computers partner with humans to accomplish tasks.
- Networking — connecting computers to each other and connecting users to computers — evolved quickly, leading to the internet and the World Wide Web, which provides access to lots of multimedia information and enables us to buy things and perform financial transactions, all online. Computers went "behind glass" again, this time in large data centers called the "cloud," which we connect to through the internet.
- As computer logic and storage became smaller and faster, it became embedded in many things around us. Now, we are surrounded by technology all the time, and, with our smartphones, we even carry computers with us wherever we go.
- Technology stares us in the face all the time, and we are surrounded by digital technology in our daily lives. When we think of technology, we usually think of computers.

CHAPTER 6

EVERYTHING IS SO COMPLEX

Life is really simple, but we insist on making it complicated.
—Confucius

SOMETIMES WE USE TERMS like "it has lots of moving parts" to characterize complexity. Those are apt words, since a complex system has many parts that work together and interact with each other in multiple ways. One part's output is input for other parts, and it is sometimes difficult to define just how the different parts interact.

Most of the high-tech devices we depend on are complex. Even if they don't contain a computer, there are lots of parts that must be designed to work correctly. When the devices contain computers, such as those in smartphones and smart speakers, the level of complexity skyrockets.

In earlier chapters, you learned that adding features to a device can increase its complexity, which can sometimes lead to it not always working correctly. You also learned that this sometimes results in our high-tech gadgets doing unexpected things. Now, we are going to dig deeper and focus on why our technology is so complex and what that means to us.

This chapter explores why everything is so complex these days, then discusses some of the problems that can arise as a result. You will hear about ideas that can be used to "hide" the complexity, as well as suggestions for making sure these complex devices are working the way they should.

Why Is Everything So Complex?

Complex systems have been around for years, but complexity today has gone from something found primarily in large systems, such as spacecraft and launch systems, supercomputers, and the electric power grid, to something that affects almost everything we touch. Most of this increase in complexity has resulted from the introduction of information technology that surrounds us at work, at home, and in our cars. This complexity has been driven by everyone's desire for more functionality and better performance, which results in more complex hardware and software and programmable devices embedded within just about everything electronic. Our dependence on technology has made us enablers for the high level of complexity that is inherent in advanced technology.

Adding capability to a device can improve how it meets user requirements, but it also adds complexity and sometimes decreases reliability. Adding additional features to a device can make it harder to use, more complex, slower, and less reliable. It makes it more difficult to navigate a large software application such as Microsoft Excel. Designers are pushed to add features to smartphones, and in the process, make those features harder to use. The more features, the more complex the smartphone. It gets harder and harder to even figure out what features are included and how to use many of them. Do users need all these features? While expecting additional features, users are also demanding that devices be easier to use and more flexible. In addition, to achieve greater reliability, there may need to be greater redundancy, error detection and correction, and backup capability, which adds still more complexity.

Key Word

Redundancy in a high-tech device means it includes additional components that provide built-in back up, so if one component fails the device keeps working. Ironically, adding redundancy makes the device more complex and, therefore, more prone to failure. So additional redundancy is not always a magic solution to improve reliability.

Without realizing it, users can easily demand new capabilities that lead to greater complexity. These demands arise from expectations that are a combination of "what we really need" and what someone has convinced us that we can't live without. Users frequently have no choice about new features because they are packaged in updated versions of a device that fix bugs in the software, and older versions of the software will eventually not be supported. We have high expectations and little patience for things that don't meet our expectations. For example, we expect smartphones, PCs, and the internet to do lots of things simultaneously, and to do it all very fast. These kinds of expectations make mobile devices and other systems more complex.

The complexity begins with the hardware, especially computer or computer-like hardware, and it extends to the software that controls the hardware. As things became "smarter," everything has become dependent on programming. Just about everything these days comes with a computer inside it, including a TV, a car (up to 100 or more computers), and even coffee makers. When a device includes a computer inside it, the term "embedded computing" is often used. The computer is part of the device, but it doesn't look like we are using a computer. An old fashioned device is designed and constructed to perform one function or several similar functions. Incorporating a computer in a device makes it more flexible and often gives it the ability to perform more functions. It can also be updated by patching the software of the internal, embedded computer.

Maybe It's the Software

The internal functioning of computer systems, including embedded computers, is driven by software. Software size has increased from thousands of "lines of code" to millions of lines of code. "Code" is a term used to describe instructions that tell a computer what to do. "Source code" is the term used for software programs written by programmers before the code is converted into "machine language," or "machine code," the bits and bytes that the hardware understands. Windows 10 is reported to have 50 million lines of source code.[117] Some cars have 100 million lines of code, which is more than the total lines of code that run on computers in some sophisticated jet airplanes.[118]

Software containing 50 million lines of code is much more complex than software with just a few thousand lines of code. It's hard to imagine millions of anything inside the devices we use every day, especially small things like smartphones. Devices have become so complex that even when good design practices are employed, the complexity can be overwhelming. In some cases, such as the software operating systems for PCs and smartphones, there may be not be a single person who knows how everything works. Operating systems are crafted by teams of programmers that can be so large the programmers don't know each other and may even be at many different locations. Each person may develop only a small part of the software, which is expected to work well in tandem with software developed by hundreds of other people. Software developers work hard to minimize the number of errors in the finished software product. Yet at the same time, they are rushing the product out the door to meet customer needs and, in some cases, to beat the competition as well. More testing before delivery of the software may uncover some of these errors. But many errors will not be discovered until after the software is in use, so it is essential to apply the latest software patches quickly after they are released to ensure that known errors are corrected. Not only will the software work better, but its vulnerability to cyberattacks will be reduced as well.

Complexity Resulting from Connectivity

I have five bars on my smartphone, but I can't seem to get my email. So maybe it's not as simple as having adequate signal strength. Welcome to the complex world of mobile computing and networking through the internet. A strong signal between a smartphone and a cell tower does not ensure that the complex configurations of computers and communications behind the scenes at the cell phone service provider and beyond are working well. We have "cell tower connectivity," but maybe not all the connectivity we need to connect to the internet using our smartphones.

There is also a lot of complexity behind the scenes when connecting to the internet using a PC or Mac. Is networking working correctly on the PC, the router, and the modem that connects to the internet service provider (ISP)? Maybe everything didn't "come back up" quite right after a momentary outage that resulted in rebooting. Is the cable working? Checking to see if the TV still works may help diagnose the situation. But just because the cable TV service is working doesn't necessarily mean that internet access is working on the cable.

What does "working" mean? The connection through the ISP's cable to the internet may be alive, but it may be working so slowly that it is not really working. Web servers may be down or the internet itself could be partly down. Connectivity to the internet is a lot more complex than it may seem, and everything must be working for users to have the usual and expected full experience.

Most homes and businesses have one connection to the internet, through one ISP, such as a cable TV provider or fiber-to-the-home service provider. Now that we are increasingly dependent on internet access from homes and business, including to control things in our homes, there may be a need for more reliable connectivity than just one connection can provide. Some providers can provide more than one cable or fiber-service connection, although this additional connection might not help if all local service from the ISP fails. Service can be purchased from more than one ISP, although the complexity of routers and other local equipment would have to increase to be able to coordinate these multiple internet-access paths. Internet access is readily available through smartphones, including support for a hotspot that essentially provides local Wi-Fi. In fact, internet access using smartphones through a cellular carrier is often fast enough and reliable enough to be the primary home internet access, or at least serve as backup internet access. Some things around the home already use cell phone service for connectivity, such as smart electric meters and some security systems.

Mobile connectivity is now supported by most cellular phone companies using 4G LTE technology, which usually provides fast data transfer and internet access, but this technology is not yet available in all areas or worldwide. I have older 3G technology in my relatively new car using a built-in cellular connection through T-Mobile, and it is very slow compared to the AT&T 4G LTE service I have on my iPhone. I have been told that the only solution to this problem is to buy a new car with a newer built-in cellular modem and, possibly, using a different service provider. The next advance in cellular service is referred to as 5G, which is predicted to roll out in 2020 and beyond.[119] Although the details of 5G are still being developed, the general goal of 5G technology is to be able to support a 1,000-fold increase in traffic, higher speeds for individual cell phones of over 10 gigabits per second, and end-to-end transmission delays of under 1 millisecond. In urban and suburban areas, 100 megabit per second communication with cell phones should be common within a decade.

Higher data rates and fewer transmission delays will help smooth access to web-based services. One way systems can be designed to provide faster apparent response, even in the face of slower network performance, is for them to "anticipate" what a user wants next and to retrieve it in advance.[120] This involves being good at "guessing" what a user is going to do next so the right thing can be downloaded in advance.

Complexity Can Lead to Glitches

In an article in *The Futurist*, Richard Vonck says, "as a general rule, the more complex something is, the more opportunity there is for it to operate in a manner other than we intended or expected."[121] As software programs grow to hundreds of thousands or millions of lines of code, they can sometimes do unexpected things. The data that controls what the software does and how it does it is usually restricted to a range of values. If data outside that range is sent to the software, it may cause it to do things that were never anticipated. This can lead to "dead ends," with software becoming hung up trying to do something but never getting there. The result may be incorrect output, or the program might crash, resulting in a device or system coming to a screeching halt or doing unusual things. This sometimes results in a need to reboot. Occasionally, even rebooting doesn't fix the problem and technical support is needed to get devices working again.

As a device becomes more complex, it becomes harder to make it work correctly all the time. Sometimes things don't appear to be working as we expect them to work. Many things are designed with a reset button to restart them in a known condition, hopefully enabling them to work correctly again. If there is no reset button or when resetting doesn't work, it may be necessary to perform the ultimate reset or reboot—unplugging the device from electrical power and plugging it back in. If the device is battery-operated, this may call for removing the battery and putting it back in. See the next chapter for everything you want to know about rebooting!

Behind the Scenes Magic

Perhaps it is amazing that our complex new technology works as well as it does. What appear to be simple tasks can be complex behind the scenes. Clicking on a link initiates a multistep process to find the web server that is home to that web page, connect to that server, and download the page to the browser on the smartphone or PC.[122] When more complicated tasks are performed, the complexity goes up, increasing the chance for things to go wrong.

A single-function product usually works well and can typically be reset or rebooted easily when it doesn't. A multifunction device, such as a PC or a smartphone, has so many moving parts that it can be difficult to get to the bottom of an apparent failure. Therefore, designers usually put many of their eggs into the reset or reboot basket—when in doubt, reboot! Preparing for a reboot requires that every function, both visible and invisible to the user, have a default starting point, which is reached by rebooting. This results in almost everything in the device being returned either to a default condition or to a start-up condition. In the process, some recent work may be lost, and it may be necessary to reconstruct some recent actions.

Many systems are multilevel or hierarchical, adding to their complexity. The levels in the hierarchy include the internet, which is accessed using a smartphone or a PC, which then connects to one or more web server computers. These remote web servers are in the cloud, in the large data centers referred to in the last chapter. In the past (and even occasionally today), users sometimes received the message "Error 404—Not Found" when they tried to access information on a remote web server. When this happened, it was difficult or impossible to tell what the problem was. Was the connection to the internet not working? If so, was that caused by a problem with the PC or smartphone, or the Wi-Fi, or the connection to the ISP? Was the internet itself disrupted, perhaps within the complicated, multilevel domain name server (DNS) system that helps locate web servers? Or was the problem in the server at the far end, the one that "hosts" the website. That server could be down or overloaded. Who would imagine the complexity that underlies such seemingly simple actions on a PC or on a smartphone?

Hiding the Complexity

The concept of hiding complexity by concealing the details enables users to focus on what's important and helps us live in a world of ubiquitous computing. We want our smartphone to "just connect" to the cloud without worrying about how it connects or where the cloud is. We want painless execution of the functions that are important, and we want to be confident that when we request a web page or other service on our smartphone it will be provided accurately, reliably, and quickly.

Usually the complexity behind how a high-tech device

responds to our requests is hidden from us, and we may not know what is going on behind the scenes. We simply trust that we will receive an accurate response. How do we know that our spreadsheet application is calculating the correct results? We could run some test cases for simple problems to check the spreadsheet's accuracy, but that would still not assure us that the spreadsheet will work correctly for all calculations. So we must take a leap of faith, accepting the spreadsheet as an old, familiar tool that we can rely on. After we have used the spreadsheet tool many times and determined the results to be accurate, we have more confidence in it.

Behind the scenes, an electronic spreadsheet stores numbers in several different formats with varying degrees of precision, such as five or seven integers followed by a decimal point and four additional digits. Any number entered or calculated within the spreadsheet is truncated or rounded to conform to the format you specify or that the spreadsheet software selects for you. Each calculation made within the spreadsheet is dependent on both software and hardware to compute the answer, rounded or truncated according to the requirements (sometimes referred to as properties) of the spreadsheet cell where the answer or result is placed.

Is this any different from how a grocery or department store computer inside the cash register adds what you owe, computing discounts and tax? How many times do you double-check the bottom line that is presented on a display or on the receipt? You may take a quick look at the receipt to make sure the bottom line is roughly as it should be based on what you bought, maybe after you leave the store. The same thing happens in a restaurant or when you buy gasoline. We have faith in the server, the cashier, the gas pump. How often do we really check the bill? Is it blind faith that makes us comfortable that the bill is correct? Yes, to some extent. A gas pump measures how many gallons of gas have flowed and multiplies this number by the price to determine what we owe. Each state or local government has an office that regularly checks each gas pump to make sure it is reasonably accurate in measuring the number of gallons, but that leaves the correct calculation of what is owed up to the operation of the internal electronic and mechanical logic of the gas pump.

If we took time to worry about the details of every transaction in our lives, we wouldn't have time to live our lives! So, hiding the complexity is essential to our well-being. Is it worth worrying about everything under the hood in our car and how it works? As long as the experience is good for us, the car runs smoothly, goes where we steer it, and gets us to our destination reliably, what more could we ask for?

As more and more technology is introduced into our lives, we are giving up knowledge and control of the details to high-tech devices. Although you can usually just assume these devices are doing everything we expect them to, it is worthwhile to ask questions from time to time about what's going on behind the scenes. If you know more, you may gain more confidence in your high-tech devices.

The complexity of our newer cars is hidden from us quite well, and gaining confidence in our cars has become harder as the number of computers in them has grown (as many as 100 computers in each high-end car), along with the millions of lines of software code that run on them. It's a little scary, too, to read about problems with this kind of software, like when some popular hybrid cars were randomly losing power and stopping on the road.[123] Experts reported that the software for this car had "spaghetti" code, which is the way unskilled programmers sometimes wrote code years ago. This kind of code has been replaced by systematic software engineering practices, which lead to more structured and reliable code that can

Do You Know What's Under the Hood?

Most of the time, we don't really want or need to know what's going on under the hood, but there are times when it is important to us. If our car's steering is not quite working as we expect it to, it may be time to ask questions, do a Google search, check the car's instruction manual, or consult a car service advisor. To know what questions to ask, we should know that the way we turn the steering wheel is only one factor that affects the car's steering. The car's stability control system, lane-keeping system, and maybe other systems also have a say in the car's steering. When these systems kick in, we may feel a little movement from time to time in the steering wheel. We should know we are feeling the movement because the car is supposed to help us steer a little bit at times.

The same thing happens when you look under the hood of computer tools you use often, such as Facebook and Google search. Do you know why only some things show up in your Facebook newsfeed, or why you are seeing certain ads? Do you know there are many ways to use Google search in addition to just inserting words in the box? If you take the time to look under the hood and find out more about the tools you use, you may be able to make things work better for you and get more out of them.

be tested more easily. One popular brand of SUV had to be recalled so updated software could be loaded (by thumb drive!) to protect its electronics against cyberattack. We have even experienced intentionally faulty software that caused cars to emit overly high emissions under normal driving conditions.[124] Protect yourself from these kinds of computer issues by responding quickly to recalls on new (and older) cars that may involve complex technology, including computer-based concerns that may affect safety.

Smart Tip

Take prompt action on car recalls, especially when they involve computer-based concerns that may affect your safety or possibly leave your car vulnerable to a cyber-attack. Be sure to act quickly for other safety recalls, too, such as air bags.

Trust But Verify

Many of the things we depend on every day are so complex that we can't just trust they will work as they should. We could just rely on blind faith, but for many high-tech things, such as software to calculate taxes, too much is at stake to just assume that they are working as we expect them to.

In the old days, when slide rules and electronic calculators were the norm, some of us used to test our high-tech devices by making calculations manually to check results. You could say we were taking a "trust but verify" approach. We can still do that with computer spreadsheets and income tax applications.

It is also possible to perform limited checks of the smart electric meter on your home to verify that it is reading the correct amount of power being used. But this can be more complicated than you may think. There may be a way to visually read out the instantaneous power consumption on the smart meter, then to turn on a power-consuming appliance and read the meter again. Or you can rely on the measurements sent in real time by the smart meter to the power company. For my home, the smart meter sends the electricity usage for each 30-minute period to the power company, and by the next day, this data is available on the power company's website. To make sure the meter is working properly, the power company can generally do a better job of testing and calibrating the smart meter than a homeowner can.

Do we have to "trust but verify" every app and device we own or might buy? Our faith that new high-tech devices are working as intended should be borne out by what we expect the devices to do and what we see them doing. But it sure would be nice to have additional confirmation that things are working correctly. I use one of the major income tax software packages, and it is tempting to rely on the bottom line it calculates for the tax due or the refund. However, I have found it helpful to review the tax forms it prepares and manually calculate some of the results to gain a better understanding of what the software is doing, which can help me make manual adjustments to the electronic worksheets and data entry forms to improve accuracy.

In the old days, some of us had checkbooks, and we calculated our running balance every time we wrote a check or made a deposit. Now, many people let the bank do it. (Not me . . . I still have a checkbook.) They take a quick look at the balance and say "it seems to be about right," then go on with their lives. Does that sound like you? You probably don't even get a paper statement anymore, so reconciling your account the old fashioned way may be difficult. You may be surprised at what you might learn if you reconcile your checkbook or use QuickBooks or whatever method you prefer to check what shows up on the bank's website, at least occasionally, to make sure everything is OK.

Likewise, it is useful to keep those little credit card receipts and check them, one by one, against what your credit card issuer shows online or on the statement they send you in the mail. You might be surprised to see that things don't always add up. Maybe the credit card company thinks you gave a lot bigger tip than the one you actually gave! Maybe an unusual charge for an online purchase has appeared out of nowhere. Maybe there is a strange charge, which may indicate that your account has been compromised. You may not need to check everything, but you should give your monthly statements more than a quick glance.

Smart Tip

Where possible, verify that your high-tech tools and devices are working correctly, especially when using them for something important.

We are relying on the cloud more and more to implement many functions, including data storage and support for communication among devices, such as iPhones and Internet of Things devices in the home. When we use an iPhone app to control a thermostat or to turn on the lights, we are going out to the cloud to a web server associated with the company that supports the devices. That web server sends control information to the thermostat, a home hub, or directly to other devices. When we use a smart speaker like an Amazon Echo, we depend on Amazon servers in the cloud to help the Echo determine what we have said, retrieve information, and create a voice response or take other actions.

How do we know the cloud is working as we expect it to? You can generally trust it, but you should check every so often to make sure it is working as advertised, such as by accessing your information in the cloud to make sure it looks OK. Yes, you should even trust and verify the cloud! Start by checking your connectivity to the cloud, perhaps by storing something there. The network connection to the data centers in the cloud may not always be working. Fortunately, many cloud applications have backups on several servers within one data center or across data centers, which, properly implemented, can increase overall reliability. For example, Google says there is a lot of data traffic between its data centers because backups are being performed most of the time. There can also be a delay, called "latency," when accessing servers and the data associated with them in the cloud. This delay can be a problem for real-time applications, such as turning on the lights on in your house, opening a door lock, or changing a thermostat setting.[125]

For many applications, the cloud service provider you use is tied to your smartphone or to an app on your smartphone. However, you may be able to select your cloud service provider for some other functions, such as backing up the files on your PC. Once you are set up with one cloud service provider, it can be difficult to move to a different one. There are likely to be inherent differences among providers and technical difficulties involved in moving your data from one to another. So, you may be locked into a cloud provider. However, that may be changing: Cisco says they are planning to provide a service to help customers move data from one cloud service to another.[126]

Will Complex Technology Ever Work Perfectly?

Internet pioneer Len Kleinrock has warned that we have reached a point where our systems are so complex that

Smart Tip

From time to time, take a look at what you have stored in the cloud, whether it is a complete backup of your iPhone or the temperature data for your fancy, high-tech home thermostat, or the video from your smart doorbell, to make sure that the data seems to be complete and makes sense.

designers can't predict how they will perform.[127] He says many systems are designed to perform very well up to some "limit" in terms of load, such as the maximum number of simultaneous users who can do typical work on the system. Once the limit is reached, access to the system can collapse, suddenly and surprisingly. If possible, a system should be designed so its performance will slowly degrade so a user can tell in advance it is about to fail. One simple example of this is a battery-powered watch that starts incrementing two seconds at a time instead of once a second when it's about time for a new battery. Modern systems and networks are usually designed so they will degrade gracefully as they become overloaded. At least, that's what they are supposed to do. But this doesn't always happen. I have spent lots of time looking at "frozen" web pages and spinning icons that are supposed to indicate something is loading! A variant of this is when nothing obvious happens after we request action, then it suddenly works.

In a practical sense, if our systems do things often that we don't expect and that we don't want them to do, we may consider them unreliable. If they just veer a little bit from the "correct answer" some of the time, we may never know there is an issue. If a car's power steering system gets it slightly wrong, we will make manual steering corrections without realizing it, just like when steering is temporarily perturbed when the car goes over a bump or pothole. The lack of a guarantee of the "correct result" all the time, in part due to complexity, can result in a lack of trust in a system, leading us to spend more time verifying results or seeking a different system.

Very few people can design computer hardware or software that works well without debugging it after it is built or programmed. There are inherent limits to the reliability of the hardware and of the software, too, as well as the overall systems. We have always had to live with occasional hardware failures. If a vacuum cleaner belt breaks or a phone line goes out for a few minutes, we can usually tolerate it, even if we don't fully understand why the failure occurred. It would be helpful to extend our patience with these kinds of failures to high-tech system and service failures. If cable TV or internet access is out for just a few minutes, our experience has led us to believe that our basically dependable service will eventually come back on without our taking action. These kinds of failures are understandable, we think, because they are familiar to us. Failure and recovery happen often enough that we feel we can cope with the situation as just another part of living in our technology-enabled world.

For important high-tech that we are dependent on, it is worth designing in high reliability. You would think the internet would have high reliability designed into everything. The internet is generally always up, and we can depend on it. But it's not nearly as reliable as the old fashioned telephone system, which we used to be so dependent on and which had an incredibly high reliability. Its reliability was said to be 99.99999 percent, known as "five nines." It almost never went down! Now, we may not have a backup for our smartphone or our PC, and we probably don't have a backup for our home connection to the internet, either. If the ISP goes down, causing our Wi-Fi to lose connectivity to the outside world, a smartphone can perform well on its own, by connecting to the internet through its cellular service provider. Many people rely solely on the cellular service provided through their smartphone or smart tablet for internet access.

ISPs and the internet "backbone" have redundancy so they can continue operating when certain types of failures occur. There have been examples of backhoes mistakenly digging up a fiber-optic cable that resulted in part of the internet going down.[128] The server farms that make up the cloud are usually redundantly connected to the internet and have redundant electrical power, which increases their availability for cloud services users. The server computers are backed up, sometimes multiple times in the same or different server farms or data centers in different parts of the world. Companies that place their web content on these servers have decisions to make, however, as to how much backup, or redundancy, they want to pay for.

Even with well-designed data centers and network connections, systems and networks can become slow and even inaccessible when everyone is trying to use them at the same time. Steps can be taken to prevent outages in this type of situation, but they don't always work. Sometimes the "load" on the systems and networks just gets heavier and heavier until everything gets clogged and stops. One kind of undesirable heavy load comes from a cyberattack known as a "denial of service" attack, in which the bad guys try to bring down a web server or other system by sending so many requests that it is overwhelmed, keeping legitimate users from accessing it.

A variant of a denial of service attack occurred in October 2016, when an attack called "Mirai" brought down servers of a company that controls some of the internet's DNS infrastructure.[129] Websites, including Twitter, the Guardian, Netflix, Reddit, and CNN, were all inaccessible.[130] This attack was reportedly caused by the takeover of certain Internet of Things devices, such as digital cameras and video recorders, turning them, collectively, into a "botnet," a set of over 100,000 maliciously attacking devices all over the Internet that were trying to connect to the same websites at the same time. These camera and recorder devices were easily taken over because they were protected only by factory-default usernames and passwords.[131] Many of these devices were especially vulnerable because the passwords were hardcoded into the firmware and couldn't be changed by the users.

The highly respected business and technology author Nicholas Carr notes that "technology improves, of course, and bugs get fixed."[132] But he says that flawlessness remains an ideal that can never be achieved. Don Norman, who has written several bestselling books about the design of things, including high-tech things, says that "the development of technology tends to follow a U-shaped curve of complexity, starting high, dropping to a low, comfortable level, and then climbing again."[133] He contends that a new technology may be complex, then as it matures, devices become simpler and more reliable. But, at a later stage, complexity again increases, perhaps as additional functions are added to improve the performance of devices.

Using Our Purchasing Power

J.D. Power, a global marketing information services company, reports on initial product quality, customer satisfaction, and buyer behavior.[134] Their reports cover the reliability of electronics and automobiles and other complex, high-tech things, and have become an incentive for manufacturers to improve

Important Resources Need More Backup

Sometimes it's necessary to keep complex, high-tech things working under very difficult conditions. When I was the chief information officer of the National Oceanic and Atmospheric Administration (NOAA), one of our priorities was to ensure that everyone could get hurricane warning information when they needed it. People needed this information when a hurricane was approaching land, but its landfall location and timing was still uncertain. The National Hurricane Center (NHC), an important part of NOAA's National Weather Service, has a web server that hosts the NHC website, which is a primary way you and I get hurricane warning information directly from the horse's mouth. In the 1990s, the NHC web server was getting busier and busier, especially as each storm approached land.

So, we created a network of backup servers at various locations that together constituted a "web farm." Each server was kept up to date with a copy of the current NHC web server content, and each server was connected to the internet in a different way and in a different part of the country. After a few years, we needed more help to meet the demands of our users. We hired a company named Akamai, which operates over 200,000 web servers[221] connected to the internet at different locations around the world, to make copies of the NHC website available to everyone, updated in real time from NHC and able to serve millions of users at the same time. All this network infrastructure is hidden from users, who just click on a link for the latest hurricane information. To this day, when a hurricane is approaching the US coastline, the NHC site becomes one of the most heavily used websites on the entire internet!

their products and services because the reports are used by consumers in their purchasing decisions. *Consumer Reports* also rates many different products based on reliability, and consumers rely on its ratings, too. Because of the availability of these kinds of reports, we realize that some products are more reliable than others. You can use these reliability reports as you compare one high-tech device to another.

Maybe we don't have to just accept unreliable performance and the need to reboot as a fact of life. Maybe there is something we can do about it, both in our selection of products and services and by encouraging manufacturers and service providers to improve quality in ways that matter to consumers. How do we band together as consumers or users to get designers and manufacturers to do a better job on reliability? That's a good question! One thing we can do is vote with our purchasing power, and buy things that are more reliable according to reports from companies like J.D. Power and *Consumer Reports*.

Systems and networks we depend on, including systems in the cloud, have many moving parts that must work together for the entire system or network to function properly. This type of complexity can lead to things not working well at times. Everything can be working well one moment, then start hiccupping and maybe even stopping altogether. The next chapter discusses how we can often recover from this kind of problem through rebooting.

Key Points

- A complex system has many parts, and the parts work together and interact with each other in multiple ways so the entire system performs tasks far better than the parts themselves could possibly do.
- Most of this complexity has resulted from the introduction of information technology that surrounds us at work, at home, and in our car.
- The software inside our high-tech devices that contain computers makes them even more complex, and, sometimes, not as dependable.
- There is also complexity behind the scenes when connecting to the internet using a PC or smartphone.
- The more complex something is, the more opportunity there is for it to operate in a manner other than we expected.
- Hiding the complexity can sometimes keep us sane. But it often helps to "look under the hood" to see whether things are running as expected.
- For things that are very important, such as taxes and bank records, it is a good idea to "trust, but verify." Try calculating a few results by hand, if you can, and compare what you get with what the tax software computes.
- For complex, high-tech systems, flawlessness remains an ideal that can never be achieved.
- Sometimes it may be necessary to get together with other users of high-tech devices and push back on designers and manufacturers to insist that things work better.

CHAPTER 7

LET'S REBOOT

MY PC IS HUNG UP AGAIN! I guess it's time to reboot! Not long ago the word "reboot" wasn't in our vocabulary. Now, every time we turn around we must reboot something to get it to work properly, or, in some cases, to get it to work at all.

You will recall from the previous chapter that complexity in our new technology systems can lead to uncertainty as to what a programmable device should do next. The system can get hung up because of software errors or when it faces input it doesn't recognize or other conditions it has never experienced. When you realize this has happened, it's time to reboot.

In this chapter, you will learn what creates the need to reboot, where the idea of rebooting came from, and how that concept is alive and well when using PCs and smartphones, and even cars. The reboot concept can be extended to the internet, too. When things go wrong as we are using the internet, we sometimes need to start over to try to make them work right again. You will also learn how to tell when a device is not working correctly and might require rebooting.

Time to Reboot

My cable box won't switch channels again. It just sits there. So, I guess it's time to reboot! This usually means finding the power plug, unplugging it, then plugging it in again, awkwardly fumbling with things behind the cable box.

My car isn't running like it should. The display panel got "stuck" as it tried to rise from the dash. I'll try closing it and opening it again, even though it is supposed to open automatically. If that doesn't work, I guess it's time to stop the car, turn the ignition off and then on again. That's how to reboot a car!

We live in an age where it seems that everything needs to be rebooted, restarted, or reset—our computers, smartphones, cable boxes, and cars. We know from first-hand experience that when something seems to be not working quite right the first thing to try is to reboot. Not only is this incessant rebooting annoying, but it takes time out of our day, time that should be devoted to work or play. Why does this happen so often, and what can we do about it?

Almost all high-tech gadgetry needs rebooting every so

Key Word

The unusual word **reboot** means to "boot up *again*" a PC, smartphone or other computer-based device. When these kinds of devices are started, their main memory is empty, so a short "bootstrap" program is loaded to boot up the device, which is then used to load more software into main memory before the computer becomes operational. A "bootstrap," for those not familiar with Western gear, is a loop in the back of a boot that is used to help pull the boot on. Rebooting is simply restarting the computer-based device, causing it to boot up again and become operational.

often to help it work well. Most of the time we sense that rebooting is needed by observing when a PC or other device has stopped or is working erratically. Some people recommend rebooting PCs, smartphones, and routers every so often just as a precaution to make sure they will work properly. Isn't there a way for advanced technology to keep things working correctly without having to reboot all the time?

Technology Is the Culprit

When we lived in a low-tech world, we never had to reboot. Rebooting was thrust on the world as it began to depend on advanced technology, especially computer technology. Things that employ advanced technology have greater functionality and are more complex than low-tech things. Plain old telephones never needed rebooting . . . or did they? When a phone couldn't get a dial tone, callers just hung it up for a few seconds and picked it up again to get a dial tone. You could say that was a form of rebooting. Electric lights, stereos, microwave ovens, and vacuum cleaners never seemed to need to be rebooted. Even cars just started up and ran, sputtering occasionally but never needing rebooting.

It is largely the complexity of advanced technology that has led to the need to reboot many of the devices we use every day. We reboot when devices no longer seem to be working properly, or when a device tells us to reboot it, or for other mysterious reasons. Sometimes the need to reboot is obvious—everything has stopped working. Sometimes the need is hidden, as things gradually stop working the way they once did and we think rebooting may restore "vitality" to the device. Are there ways we can avoid rebooting, making us happier and more productive? Or is there something inherent about new technology that makes rebooting an ever-present need as part of the care and feeding of our technological partners?

It All Started with the PC

Perhaps it all started with control-alt-delete. Holding all three keys down at the same time on an IBM-style PC interrupts what your PC is doing. This "get out of jail" key combination on a PC either restarts the software operating system or takes the user to a short list of options for stopping tasks and other things, depending on the version of Windows that is running.

For the Tech Curious

The term "reboot" was thrust upon us with the advent of the personal computer. We didn't understand what it meant to reboot or why we had to do it so often. The geeky three button mantra "control-alt-delete" for PCs made it seem mysterious, like something we shouldn't question or understand. In 1981, a programmer named David Bradley was part of a team working on the new IBM personal computer.[222] Bradley and the other programmers were encountering programming glitches as they tested new software and, as a result, they needed to restart the computer often. But turning the machine off and back on again initiated a series of memory tests that took an unacceptably long time. So Bradley created control-alt-delete so he and the other programmers could restart the computer without time-consuming memory tests. This new shortcut restart wasn't intended for use by anyone other than the programmers, and they used it only because the hardware guys couldn't or wouldn't add a special key to the keyboard for rebooting. It was a temporary shortcut to make debugging more efficient, by avoiding a full reboot with time-consuming system testing at startup. It was not until 2013 that Bill Gates publicly admitted that control-alt-delete was a mistake![223]

When the IBM PC was introduced in fall 1981, few people were aware of control-alt-delete. But in the early 1990s, even after the introduction of Microsoft Windows to replace the Disk Operating System (DOS), Windows would crash frequently, leading to the infamous DOS blue screen that meant the system had crashed. The way out was to hit control-alt-delete, for a fast, "soft" restart or reboot of the PC.

Key Words

A **soft reboot**, sometimes called a **warm reboot**, is when a device is restarted without turning the power off, and in the process, the device's software is reinitialized. A **hard reboot**, sometimes called a **cold reboot**, is when a device is powered down before it is turned on again.

Today, control-alt-delete is still alive and well in Windows 10. Hitting control-alt-delete stops normal Windows execution and gives the user several choices, such as to lock the PC or start the task manager. When a program running on a PC stops working, hitting control-alt-delete takes a user to the task manager and makes it possible to stop just that program without having to reboot the entire PC.

For PCs, there is also an option in the Start menu to Restart, which is a soft reboot, a "graceful" shutdown followed by a quick boot up, which usually saves all the ongoing work. Finally, when all else fails, pressing the PC's power button and holding it down for several seconds will shut down the PC.

Pressing the PC's power button again, for just a second or so, brings the PC back to life, and you will have completed a hard reboot. If cleanup is needed resulting from the unusual shutdown, it is done automatically when Windows starts, taking a little longer than normal. It is possible that some changes made to files since the last startup will be lost, so files should be saved fairly often, and, if possible, just before pressing the button on the PC to turn it off rather than asking Windows to shut it down gracefully.

Apple Macs, known for their clean and user-friendly interface, also have reboot options because they, too, can get hung up. The Mac has a reboot function as a top menu option. It also has a control-eject, two-key reboot that is Apple's equivalent for the PC's control-alt-delete. And, when all else fails, the power button should be pressed for several seconds until the Mac shuts down. You can then power back up again, but unsaved work is likely to be lost with this approach.

Mobile Devices Are Not Immune

My smartphone occasionally becomes slow, and it sometimes hangs up. I can try deleting the working copies of the open apps to minimize the workload on the smartphone, but that doesn't always work for apps that may not be working correctly. However, the manufacturer built in a reboot capability just in case it is needed.

Yes, smartphones have to rebooted, too! They contain one or more powerful microprocessors and other complex hardware, as well as millions of lines of software. So they are vulnerable to losing their way from time to time, just like PCs. The problem is compounded because much of the software we depend on as we use our smartphones is contained in apps, which are developed by a wide variety of individuals and organizations and subjected to much less testing and scrutiny than the operating system software, which is developed and supported by the smartphone manufacturer.

How to Reboot a Smartphone

Some smartphones have reboot functions that are engaged by pressing or pointing to buttons. An iPhone 8 and an iPhone X can be restarted by quickly pushing and releasing the volume up button, then quickly pushing and releasing the volume down button, then pressing and holding the power button on the right side until the Apple logo appears on the screen. Don't get distracted when the power-off "slider" appears on the screen. Just keep holding the power button down.

An Android phone can be rebooted by holding down the power button for one to two seconds until a small window appears with a menu. On some Android phones you will need to push the volume button along with the home button to bring up the reboot menu. Just pick restart from the menu, and your Android device will restart (a soft reboot). If that doesn't work, hold the power button down for 10 seconds or so until the screen goes off and the phone shuts down. Then hold down the power button again until it restarts. On some Android phones, you will need to push the volume button and the power button at the same time for more than seven seconds to make them restart. If that still doesn't work, you can remove the battery and reinsert it for a cold reboot. You can always Google your brand and smartphone model to find out exactly how to reboot it.

Even Internet Access May Need Rebooting Help

When internet access fails, the problem can be related to any of several different things. The problem might be with internet access equipment in your home. If you have a separate cable modem and router, the problem can sometimes be fixed by turning off the modem and the router for several seconds, then turning them back on. With a router separate from the modem, it is usually recommended that the modem be powered on before the router, although it doesn't always matter. If that doesn't work, the router may need to be reset, either a minimal reset or a full reset, which returns the router to the factory settings. On some routers, there is a reset button on the back. Instructions vary as to how long to hold the reset button down. But be careful doing this! For some routers, holding the button down for 10 seconds or longer takes the device back to its original state, and it may be necessary to manually reload settings, such as the router password and, if the router includes Wi-Fi, the wireless network name and password, and type of encryption used.

Some internet connections, such as Fios, use a "gateway," which combines a modem and a Wi-Fi router. Turning a gateway off may not be possible, since it may have an internal battery backup, so it may be necessary to press the reset button, maybe just a short, two- to three-second push. If that still doesn't work, it may be necessary to call the ISP and have them check the status of the line and the gateway from their end.

Or the problem may be with your PC or smartphone or other device you are using to try to reach the internet. If you're not sure what is causing the problem, hit control-alt-delete to stop the task running on your PC, or try to stop an app that may have hung up your smartphone. If that doesn't help, you can try restarting or rebooting the PC or smartphone. If things still aren't working, reboot the router and modem or the gateway if you are connected through these devices. Still stuck? Wait and try again later. That strategy sometimes works.

Internet-access problems can also be cloud-based. For example, a PC or a smartphone may be connected to a website running on a computer server in the cloud when it stops

Key Words

ISPs provide several kinds of equipment to connect your home to the internet. A **modem** connects the home to the cable and provides a digital connection for a router. A **router** connects one or more hardwired devices to the modem, helping them all to work at the same time. Many routers are **Wi-Fi-enabled**, which means they create a home Wi-Fi as well as connect hardwired devices. A **gateway** combines a modem and router in one box, which connects to the cable on one side and to PCs and other home hardwired devices on the other side. Using built-in Wi-Fi, the gateway also connects to wireless devices like smartphones and smart pads. In the case of Verizon Fios, the gateway can also be used to connect a telephone to the fiber-optic cable, and there will be another box, an Optical Network Terminal that is attached to a wall either outside or inside your house, which connects your TVs and router to the fiber-optic cable.

getting a response from the server. How are things reset in the cloud, or even in a single server computer that is somewhere on the internet? Unfortunately, there is no internet reset function, partly because many factors can cause these kinds of problems. Maybe the remote server is down. Maybe the data center is down or disconnected from the internet. It happens. Not all web servers are customer-friendly enough to send a temporary "I'm down" message. The server could be undergoing emergency maintenance, especially if it's happening at a time of day when the server is usually up and running. Perhaps the server has an internal problem and needs to be rebooted. Perhaps a cyberattack is causing the problem. We will probably never know unless the problem is widespread enough to attract the attention of the news media.

We can try to "fix" these kinds of problems by closing our browser and opening it again, then relinking to the website. This may work right away. If it doesn't, try to access another website to make sure your PC or smartphone and browser are working. If they are, it's usually best to wait 5 or 10 minutes or longer and try to access the website again.

Our Cars May Need Rebooting Too

Cars are not exempt from rebooting, either, but it is not usually thought of as rebooting. How is a car rebooted? If the problem is with the navigation or entertainment system, try pressing a few buttons to start a different function, such as hitting the radio button. Then go back to navigation and you may find everything suddenly working as expected. If things really go out of whack, it may be necessary to recycle the engine by turning the ignition off, then restarting the engine, which usually resets all the car's computers and associated

Smart Tip

Chances are, at some point, you will need to reboot your high-tech devices, so be prepared by learning now how to reboot them. You can Google for instructions for your specific device.

equipment. This extreme measure can take a minute or two before everything is up and running again — obviously a major reboot!

Grin and Bear It

It looks like rebooting will be with us for the indefinite future, and we will just have to live with it until designers and manufacturers get a lot smarter and fix most of the problems that lead to the need to reboot. But that's not going to happen any time soon.

My personal experience is that you have to reboot so often with so many of the high-tech devices that it becomes second nature, just part of the inconvenience we put up with to reap the benefits of new technology.

Remember, rebooting is nothing new. We did it with our

For the Tech Curious

One solution to having to minimize our need to reboot all the time is to have our high-tech devices reboot themselves! Our PC or smartphone may sense that it needs to be rebooted, and it may do this without our even realizing it, either on its own or at the direction of some person or process out on the internet. Automatic rebooting requires that a device "self-realize" that it is out of control, in an infinite loop, or doing something illogical, which requires initiating a reboot. A reboot may be forced on your device after a software update has been downloaded and installed and it then requires a reboot to be fully installed. Even then, a PC usually asks us whether we are ready for it to reboot. A smartphone, however, may just reboot on its own, since it may not be possible to use the smartphone until after it is rebooted.

old telephones if a call didn't go through or when we got a strange beeping signal after dialing a number. We are just doing something similar in a modern context, with all our various devices and just about everything else that goes beep and bonk around us.

Rather than being frustrated, we could look at it this way: Like us, our technology just needs to be "rejuvenated" occasionally to be able to work properly again. In fact, so many things need rebooting from time to time that it is fair to say that we live in a "reboot world"!

Now that we have identified rebooting as one way to cope with the inevitable problems that complexity has brought us, it is time to explore a whole new world that makes our technology even more complex. Turn the page, and let's dig into the Internet of Things.

Key Points

- Every time we turn around we must reboot something to get it to work properly, and in some cases, to get it to work at all.
- The word "reboot" means to boot up a stopped PC, smartphone, or other computer-based device and get it running again.
- We live in an age where it seems that everything needs to be rebooted, restarted, or reset — our computers, smartphones, cable boxes, and cars.
- It is largely the complexity of advanced technology that has led to the need to reboot many of the devices we use every day.
- To reboot a PC, you can perform a soft reboot by going to the Start menu and clicking on "Restart." Smartphones can be rebooted too, by pressing various combinations of buttons, depending on the brand and model. Sometimes a car requires rebooting by turning the engine off and back on again.
- When your access to a website on the internet doesn't seem to be working, close the web browser and reopen it, then try to link to the website again.
- It looks like rebooting will be with us for the indefinite future, with all types of high-tech devices, and we will just have to live with it.

CHAPTER 8

THE THINGS ARE COMING!

NOW THAT NEW TECHNOLOGY has become so complex that many of the devices we depend on need to be rebooted all too often, high-tech developers may have found a way to make our world still more complex. It is called the Internet of Things (IoT). The IoT is the concept of making physical things around us smart and connecting them to each other and, through the internet, to the cloud. Ordinary physical things around the home, at work, in factories, in stores, around our cities, and in our cars (including cars themselves) have begun to "come alive" and be part of our new technology world.

The IoT is where the physical world meets the digital world—and it's growing by leaps and bounds. The Gartner Group predicts that there will be 25 billion IoT-connected devices by 2021.[135] Many of these will be part of the IoT in our homes. As consumers buy more and more appliances, entertainment, and other smart-home devices that include internet connectivity, especially as they replace older devices, the home market is projected to pick up.[136]

The primary focus of this chapter is on how the IoT is helping you at home and how you can get more out of it and better enjoy its benefits. Some background and examples are included to put home IoT into context relative to how it is taking the whole world by storm, including factories, distribution centers, and health care. A little history of IoT helps tell the story, including how the concept of "computing everywhere" was created. Finally, you'll also find tips for successful do-it-yourself IoT installation, although you need to buy online services tied to specific IoT products to make them work. And for those with neither the time nor the DIY inclination, buying help to install home IoT is also discussed.

How Did IoT Become a Big Deal?

Relatively simple automation at home and at work and elsewhere has been around for a long time. For example, we have had centralized systems for lighting control, where one switch controls lots of lights, turning them on and off and dimming them, and we have had thermostats that can have different temperature settings for day and night. We have had doors that open when we get near them and garage door openers that work by remote control from our cars. The technology for RFID tags (which is used to track merchandise in stores and warehouses) and for E-ZPass transponders in cars (which makes electronic fee collection possible) has been available for 40 years. Robots with sensors that help locate and pick up things have been in factories for over 50 years. These are all precursors to the IoT.

Key Word

Radio frequency identification system (RFID) is a technology that enables computer-connected sensors to identify objects and record data about them using radio signals bounced off objects with RFID tags.

Key Word

E-ZPass is one type of automated toll collection system on highways, bridges, and tunnels that identifies cars with E-ZPass RFID tags and charges tolls by deducting the charge from a pre-paid account.

In 1988, a researcher at Xerox PARC named Mark Weiser must have seen the electronic writing on the wall when he coined the term "ubiquitous computing," which means there will be computing everywhere.[137] He probably had something like the IoT in mind when he said that "[computers] weave themselves into the fabric of everyday life until they are indistinguishable from it."

As the IoT has appeared in our lives over the last several years, computer-like capability has been added to many things around us. The IoT idea has gained steam as electronics and computers have become much more capable, smaller, and less expensive. Many of these things have embedded computers, which were discussed in Chapter 6. Some also contain sensors that detect whether someone is nearby (occupancy sensors), what the temperature is, or how much light there is. Most of these things are connected to other things and to the internet using Wi-Fi or some other form of wireless networking. Some perform tasks, like locking a door, switching on a light, or turning on an appliance like a coffee maker.

A lot of things are often tied to the IoT banner. The National Institute of Standards and Technology (NIST), for example, includes the IoT in a broad category of systems that it calls "cyber-physical systems," which are "co-engineered interacting networks of physical and computational components."[138]

NIST focuses on these systems as the foundation for the nation's critical infrastructure, expecting that these systems "will bring advances in personalized health care, emergency

Not Just for the Home

Although we will be focusing on the IoT at home, let's take a moment to tour the IoT elsewhere in our lives. Here are some other places where the IoT is being deployed.

- *Industrial Applications*: The IoT is found on the factory floor and in distribution centers, with robotic arms and other manipulators used to assemble and paint cars and many other tasks. In distribution centers, picking and moving things around and even packing boxes is heavily automated, with robots on wheels and, sometimes, with manipulators attached.
- *Health Care*: Many of the devices used in hospitals to monitor the condition of patients, to control delivery of IVs, and to scan patients' bodies are computer-based, and they are often networked to other hospital systems. In doctors' offices, the doctors and nurses sit in front of their PCs or smart tablets and enter patient information, order tests and prescriptions, and keep track of patients' health-care records.
- *Personal Care*: Wherever we are, we wear fitness trackers and electronic watches that are connected to the internet. We want to know how many steps we have taken and if our vital signs are OK, and, if they are not, to connect us with someone who can help us. We use safety monitors to make sure our elderly family members are up and around when they should be and taking their pills as they should. We want them to be connected all the time and to be able to call for help.

response, traffic flow management, and electric power generation and delivery."

The IoT at Home

The IoT is quickly becoming a presence in many of our homes as we add more automation to home functions like security, heating, lighting, and entertainment systems. At home, smartphones are being used to control smart devices such as thermostats and lighting.

Over the last decade, we have become much more aware of the smart things around us. TVs and appliances are smart; they include embedded computers and can be connected to the internet. We have become increasingly aware that there are more and more sensors everywhere. Many of these sensors are part of our TVs, smartphones, and smart thermostats, and are most likely sharing personal information on the internet about our habits and whereabouts. Perhaps the IoT is the wrong name for this phenomenon. Some people suggest it should be called the "Internet of Sensors."

Can You Tell What's Smart?

Do you know which things around you are "smart"? Can you tell by looking whether a clock is just a clock or if it is connected to the internet or to a satellite with a very accurate clock, so it keeps especially good time? Is the speaker sitting on a table just there to play music, or is it is a smart speaker that is listening for you to give it commands? Look around the room. Now go into another room. You may be surprised at how many things have become "smart" recently. Even your washer and dryer may be connected to the internet.

DIY Is All the Rage

The trend over the last decade has been toward do-it-yourself home IoT. It is relatively simple for people to buy and set up one or two IoT devices, then a few more, until they wind up with enough so they make life more interesting and fun. Smart devices for home IoT are in stores such as Home Depot or Best Buy and on online shopping sites like Amazon. And some companies that already have a foot in the door in your home would like to support some of your IoT as well. Comcast, for example, has a "Works with Xfinity" home automation partner program, and they also offer an Xfinity Home Security service.

It is now much easier than in the past to use off-the-shelf gizmos to control heating and air conditioning and to open and close garage doors. Lights can easily be turned on and off and dimmed, smart electric outlets can control power to whatever is plugged into them, and smart doorbells and smart speakers are good DIY projects for the home. Individual devices are usually easy to install and set up, even in large numbers, but you can often purchase installation help for individual devices when you buy them.

If you are considering hopping on the DIY bandwagon, you probably have a Wi-Fi router at home that is connected to

Smart Tip

Before you take on the whole house with smart things everywhere, start small and get your feet wet with just a few IoT devices at home. That will let you can gain experience and become comfortable with how they work and what they can do for you.

the internet, and you likely use it to connect your smartphones to the internet when you are home. Most home IoT devices can also be easily connected to your home Wi-Fi.

In general, setting up IoT devices yourself is easy to do. You just plug an Amazon Echo into an electrical outlet, for example, then download the Alexa app to your smartphone. You then follow the instructions you receive on your smartphone and by audio from Alexa to connect the Echo to your Wi-Fi and you can start asking your Alexa, the voice of your Echo, to do things for you. Setting up smart electrical outlets is done in a similar way, and they can be controlled by talking to Alexa if you set them up using your Echo.

Some devices, such as the Nest and Ecobee smart thermostats, are a little more complicated. You need to remove your old thermostat from the wall, carefully keeping track of the wires, then connect them to the new thermostat following the manufacturer's instructions. You then follow the instructions to connect the thermostat to your Wi-Fi so it will work correctly with your furnace and air conditioner and be accessible to your smartphone so you can control it remotely.

For the Tech Curious

It is useful to know what frequency bands and Wi-Fi types your router supports. Most Wi-Fi devices operate on the 2.4 GHz frequency band, and they may also operate on the 5 GHz band, which supports faster speeds and greater distances. Most IoT devices work fine at 2.4 GHz, so long as they aren't too far away from the router. Routers come in different models, too. The faster ones meet industry standards IEEE 802.11n and IEEE 802.11ac. When devices conform to industry standards, they can work together.

Where It All Began

It all started a couple of decades ago with a two-prong approach to home automation. The approach selected by most folks in those days was DIY-based, such as "X-10" technology that used home electrical wiring for the signals that controlled lights and other devices. Some advanced functionality was possible with PC-based software and specialized controllers, such as setting different "scenes" for combinations of lighting (think dimmed or bright). The other approach was a high-end home automation solution, exemplified by Crestron, a company that makes commercial building and home automation systems. These high-end systems, installed and maintained by experts, are still available, and they can support lighting, whole-home audio, heating and air conditioning, opening and shutting drapes and shades, and home security.

Home automation is transitioning from high-end systems to less expensive ones that can be installed more easily. The older, high-end systems usually required a lot of wiring throughout the home and a closet or room with a rack or two of equipment to control everything. But we now live in a wireless world, one in which relatively inexpensive wireless, off-the-shelf home automation and audio/video components are dominating home automation installations.

This transition to wireless is especially exciting if you want high-quality sound around your house. The industry went from complex, whole-home, wired audiophile systems to high-quality wireless audio components connected through the internet to audio streaming sources. These DIY systems are typified by companies like Sonos, perhaps the best-known brand of high-quality, wireless, multiroom home sound systems. However, for true-blue audiophiles, who still need their big, booming speakers, fancy tuners, and amplifiers, these high-quality sound solutions may not fit the bill.

That way, you can control the temperature when you are awake, asleep, and away from home, as well as other thermostat functions. These thermostats are connected to their manufacturer's servers on the internet, and, as a result, they automatically receive software updates.

It pays to read the instructions that come with smart thermostats, especially the details of electrical connections to the heating and air conditioning system. Also keep in mind that the thermostat on the wall is a lot more than a simple light switch. You certainly don't want your heat to come on for a long time and not go off! That could be hazardous to you and your home. Sometimes, home heating and air conditioning contractors will try to talk you out of DIY smart thermostats, because they can usually provide products that can do at least part of the job of a smart thermostat and they feel more comfortable servicing those devices.

Another kind of home IoT device that you may find in stores is called a "hub." It connects to your Wi-Fi and to some of your devices, and it can be used to control them, even when they use different networking protocols, which is how computer-type devices talk with each other. For example, many network-connected electronic locks use the Z-Wave protocol. I can tell Alexa to lock the door, and the Amazon Echo talks with my hub through the internet and my Wi-Fi, and the hub then sends a signal to lock the door. Hubs can be a little more difficult to set up than typical IoT devices, and they add complexity to a home IoT setup. Also, Amazon Echo can now perform some of the same functions as a hub, such as turning lights on and off on a preset schedule. However, if you envision a large, complicated home IoT installation with devices from many different vendors, you may want to consider a hub to help everything work well together.

Appliances Are Getting Smarter

The world of home appliances is fast becoming part of the IoT, too. Some newer appliances can connect to the internet through your Wi-Fi so the manufacturer can run remote testing and diagnosis problems. Your appliances can even call for maintenance when necessary. Some washers and dryers can notify you by smartphone when your load is done.

Smart appliances have greater functionality and more buttons and instructions to follow, so they are sometimes harder to use than their old fashioned counterparts. However, this isn't always true. Users may be able to select default combinations of functions easily by pressing just a few buttons.

Many Devices Need External Support

You may be able to set up home automation devices on your own, but many of them are controlled by and dependent on internet support provided by the manufacturer. And some of these services have to be paid for, such as video data storage for Ring doorbells. What happens when the manufacturer's service goes down and you lose the video of a package thief at the front door?

Most of these devices can operate on their own for a while, and this kind of service seldom goes down for a long time. But this dependency on remote, manufacturer-provided services can make someone think twice about buying some IoT devices. What happens when a manufacturer stops supporting the thermostat model you have? Experience so far has shown that most older models are still supported, but what if a manufacturer goes out of business? I don't think this has happened recently; however, companies do get bought by other companies. Nest is now owned by Google, for example. And Ring is now owned by Amazon.

Smart Tip

Be sure to ask lots of questions when you are considering a new IoT device. Google the device and read reviews. Be sure you understand whether the device requires continued service through the internet and what that might cost you.

Securing Your IoT Devices

From a cybersecurity viewpoint, each IoT device connected to the internet could potentially become a point of entry for hackers.[139] Many IoT devices lack basic cybersecurity protection, giving adversaries more opportunities to penetrate and compromise IT systems and introduce problems. It is possible that all the connected things in a house might get a virus because one connected thing has weak security and is compromised by a cyberattack through the internet.

Smart devices can be more vulnerable to cyberattacks than PCs and smartphones, and the vulnerability increases when the device's programming, usually stored as firmware, cannot be updated with current cybersecurity protection. Most of these devices have no software operating system or just a

Computing on the Edge

When experts look at the IoT big picture, they are concerned that the internet might become overwhelmed from the millions of devices transmitting data to server computers for processing and storage. Among other problems, this logjam may result in service delays.

This expectation has led to the concept of edge computing, in which some of the computing and storage are located at the "edge" of the cloud, perhaps in equipment provided by an ISP or by using other equipment located in homes, offices, and factories. Edge computing has been proposed as a way of dealing with extremely large amounts of data sent to and stored in the cloud. Cisco has developed a concept for edge computing called "fog computing."[224] With fog computing, the most time-sensitive data is analyzed at the network edge, close to where the data is generated, instead of being sent through the internet to servers in the cloud. Cisco's use of the term "fog" is a catchy way of making an analogy from what we call an atmospheric cloud when it is near the ground.

Edge computing can help with latency issues, including potential unacceptable delays in accessing service in the cloud. Video cameras and other sensors that operate continually can result in a substantial data stream. Even backing up a smartphone can require transferring a lot of data. Apple limits transfers of iPhone photos to its cloud by "metering" the data transfer. Only so many pictures per hour or day can be transferred to keep the network and the Apple cloud from being overwhelmed.

The issue of managing billions of sensors and other devices needs to be addressed. As the IoT becomes larger and larger, the complexity of everything can grow enormously.

minimal one, and they have minimal defense against cyberattacks. Many times their connections to each other and the outside world are not encrypted, and, of course, users sometimes take the path of least resistance as they set up IoT networks, including using default user IDs and passwords, even when they are able to change them.

A *USA Today* article quotes an HP security research study which concludes that "70 percent of the most commonly used Internet of Things devices had serious security flaws."[140] These kinds of flaws include passwords that are often fixed by the manufacturer and can't be changed, leading to events like the massive, partial internet outage across part of the US in October 2016. The attackers used a "distributed denial of service" attack against internet infrastructure, which blocked access to several major websites in the US and Europe. The attack was made possible by hackers who took over unprotected IoT devices, including security cameras and DVRs, then turned millions of these devices into "bots," under the control one or more attackers somewhere in the world.[141]

The same *USA Today* article offered some helpful suggestions for improving IoT security, such as not storing personally identifying information on any device.[142] It also recommended using a unique and complex password for each device and reading the fine print to find out what information is gathered

Key Word

Bots are IoT devices or PCs that have been taken over by attackers and are being used as "robots" to carry out cyberattacks.

and stored by each device and shared with the cloud-based support service operated by the device manufacturer or a third party. It also includes the very important recommendation of not using default usernames and passwords.

The Department of Homeland Security has issued guidance on IoT security that focuses on doing the best we can given the limitations of current IoT devices, until they become better engineered from a cybersecurity standpoint.[143] The Department's US Computer Emergency Readiness Team (US-CERT) recommends that you evaluate the security settings of all IoT devices to ensure the strongest possible security, keep the software on all IoT devices updated with the latest patches, consider part-time connectivity to the internet to reduce risk, and use strong passwords to protect IoT devices, when possible.

A Federal Trade Commission (FTC) report on privacy and security of the IoT warned that data sent by home IoT devices can "provide a window into the previously private home."[144] The report states that "security vulnerabilities in camera-equipped devices have also raised the specter of spying in the home," citing a CNN report in which a security vulnerability (now reported to be patched) in Samsung smart TVs "enabled hackers to remotely turn on the TVs' built-in cameras without leaving any trace of it on the screen."[145] Both CBS News and the BBC have reported on incidents in which a hacker was able to remotely control the camera on a baby monitor and talk to the baby.[146] A 2018 report in the *Washington Post* summarized an experience in which a baby monitor started beeping, then "spouting sexual expletives." After the parents turned on the light in the baby's room, a Nest camera in the same room started talking in a man's voice, telling them to turn the lights back off. He also said, "I'm going to kidnap your baby" and "I'm in your baby's room."[147] A principal culprit in these cases was apparently the use of default passwords on the camera systems, and possibly a home Wi-Fi that was not adequately encrypted.

The FTC report cited above urges businesses to protect the privacy and security of consumers who use products that are part of the IoT. The FTC recommends that companies build security into their IoT devices in the initial development stage, rather than as an afterthought. It also suggests that IoT device designers take advantage of what experts have already learned about security, including the use of strong encryption and changeable passwords.

These FTC recommendations are directed to companies that design, manufacture, market, and support IoT devices, not to all of us who use these gizmos. But we are the ones who are most affected, so we need to make sure we buy products that follow these recommendations and provide feedback to companies that don't. A practical way to evaluate these kinds of devices is by learning more about these products on consumer websites.

Some ISPs have begun to help customers with IoT security. For example, Verizon Fios customers are now provided with a new service called Verizon Home Network Protection, which provides some kinds of needed cybersecurity protection for IoT at home, such as shutting down devices that may be transmitting too much data to the internet or preventing cyberattackers from reaching some IoT devices.

Another way you could prevent IoT devices from compromising other devices at home is to set up two home networks, one for IoT devices and one for PCs and mobile devices. The easiest way to set up two separate networks is to use the "guest network" feature of many Wi-Fi routers or gateways. Each Wi-Fi network should have its own unique name and password, and each should use good encryption, such as WPA2, which is an option that can be selected during Wi-Fi setup, as described in Chapter 4. As with all high-tech devices, the software of all IoT devices should be kept up to date and protected from viruses and malware, to the extent they are able to incorporate such protection.

Smart Tip

Try to buy IoT devices with built-in security that is updated automatically as cyber threats change and new software vulnerabilities are discovered. Ask questions about security when buying IoT devices.

The IoT at home represents an opportunity for us to exploit new technology to help us in our daily lives. This kind of new technology can help us in meaningful ways every day, although we need to take steps to protect our security when using them. It's worth trying the DIY route when installing these devices, knowing you can often get help from stores, online sources, or manufacturer or retail phone hotlines. In the next chapter, you will read about some of the things you can do to survive all this new technology at the same time you benefit from it.

Key Points

- The Internet of Things is the concept of making physical things around us smart and connecting them to each other and, through the internet, to the cloud.
- Computer-like capability has been added to many things around us over the last several years, as the IoT has appeared in our lives. The IoT idea has gained steam as electronics and computers have become much more capable, smaller, and less expensive.
- In addition to our homes, the IoT is found in industrial applications on the factory floor and in distribution center operations. It is also found in hospitals, doctors' offices, and other places.
- The IoT is quickly becoming a presence in many of our homes as we add more automation to home functions like security, heating, lighting, and entertainment.
- "Do it yourself" works well for home IoT technology. Many people buy and set up one, two, or more IoT devices that make life more interesting and fun.
- Many home IoT devices are dependent on control and other support provided by manufacturer-provided internet services.
- Try to buy IoT devices with built-in security that is updated automatically as cyber threats change and new software vulnerabilities are discovered. Ask questions about security when buying IoT devices.

CHAPTER 9

HOW TO SURVIVE NEW TECHNOLOGY

WE HAVE ALREADY COVERED a lot of ground, giving you many tips and tactics for surviving, enjoying, and benefiting from new tech. In this chapter, we will add to your repertoire, but the emphasis will be on surviving, because if we're not careful, our tech can rule the roost and we can get lost in this new high-tech world.

So, in this chapter, you will find ideas for avoiding information overload, which can happen a lot easier than in the past. After all, when your smartphone puts a world of knowledge at your fingertips, it can be hard to block the torrent of information that sometimes flows your way. You'll also find advice on how to avoid being overwhelmed by too much technology, so you ensure that *you* are in charge in your life, not your high-tech gizmos—and my favorite: "simplify, simplify, simplify" our lives and our use of technology.

Watch Out for Information Overload

All day long we are subjected to a barrage of information. Emails! Texts! Notifications from Facebook and news sites! Smartphones are binging and buzzing all around us. When you receive a phone call, do you immediately answer it, or do you first look to see who is calling? Do you know that it's perfectly OK to not answer and send the call to voicemail if it doesn't seem to be an urgent call? A little self-discipline in answering calls and responding to emails and texts can help put you back in charge of your day, which can help your life run more smoothly and productively. Otherwise, you may be doomed to live a life of continual disruptions.

I haven't mentioned other sources of information that we may also want to throttle back a bit. TVs and radios blare at us when they are turned on. Newspapers and magazines are quieter, but they can stack up, waiting for us to read them. A pile of incoming letters and other things in our physical inbox at work and in our mailbox at home adds to the flow of information we have to deal with every day.

Perhaps you are an information-overload enabler, as I sometimes am. Most mornings I check my favorite news sites and financial sites for the latest scoop before I get myself going, and, of course, I also check for texts and emails that may have arrived during the night. I sometimes watch too many TV news shows, too. I read two hard-copy newspapers that are delivered each morning, although I rarely get to anything

Driven to Distraction

Information overload can lead to anxiety, loss of creativity, and lower productivity in individuals. An article in *The Economist* offers three reasons why information overload can be a serious problem. First, it can make people anxious, because it can lead to a buildup of more stress hormones. Second, creativity can be reduced when incoming information interrupts an individual's focus. And finally, productivity can be reduced if information overload leads to undertaking multiple tasks in parallel, because people make more errors and become less productive when they multitask.[225]

but the headlines until later in the day. I don't always check my smartphone whenever it beeps, but I usually check it within an hour or so of any notification. Sometimes when I am waiting for something, like for coffee at Starbucks, I will idly browse my smartphone, scrolling through email, texts, Facebook, the stock market, and news apps. I love to Google people and stories and other things when they come to my attention from any source, which can lead to a chain of searches about people, companies, and products. I don't consider my daily intake of information to be information overload. But what is comfortable for me might be too much for someone else. It's important to know yourself and your own preferences for the amount and kinds of information you would like to come your way each day.

Can You Believe Everything You Read on the Internet?
With so much information thrown at us all the time, we need to be more skeptical about the information we receive. We have all learned, sometimes the hard way, that what we see on the internet may not be true. The same goes for TV. Even if an article looks factual or truthful, it may be biased, intentionally or unintentionally. A significant part of the information we view on the internet has to be read with care and interpreted

For the Tech Curious

What is the difference between data and information? Data are unorganized bits and bytes. When data is organized and processed or interpreted so it is useful, information is generated. Some people carry all this a step or two further, saying that information leads to knowledge, often with the help of other input, and that leads to wisdom.[226]

Data by the Numbers

There is more information today than ever before, but information overload is not a new thing, brought about by smartphones and the web. Long before the internet, humankind suffered from information overload. According to J. Peder Zane, writing in the *New York Times*, "at least since the heyday of ancient Greece and Rome, each generation has confronted the overwhelming struggle to search, sift, and sort growing piles of information to make what is known useful."[227] In the Middle Ages humans invented indexes and tables of contents, and, during the Age of Enlightenment, encyclopedias were developed. Zane notes that "by the 20th century, the storehouse of useful knowledge had grown at such an alarming rate that the possibility of mastering just one area of study, such as physics, literature, or art became less aspiration than delusion." Yet it wasn't until 1970 that Alvin Toffler popularized the term "information overload.[228]

As we examine the amount of data that is inundating us now, it will help to know some of the unusual words that have been used to describe large amounts of data. These words start with a "bit," which is "binary digit." A bit can have a value of either zero or one. Next comes a byte, which is usually 8 bits. And . . .

- A kilobyte (KB) is a thousand bytes.
- A megabyte (MB) is a thousand kilobytes.
- A gigabyte (GB) is a thousand megabytes.
- A terabyte (TB) is a thousand gigabytes.
- A petabyte (PB) is a thousand terabytes.
- An exabyte (EB) is a thousand petabytes.
- And a zettabyte (ZB) is a thousand exabytes.

The largest storage device on a PC or laptop, usually a hard disk drive, contains several hundred or more gigabytes of storage. PCs also have 2 to 16 gigabytes of random access memory (RAM), which is much faster than hard disk memory but loses its content when the power is turned off. An iPhone and an iPad typically have 16 to 256 gigabytes of storage, using flash memory, which is solid state memory that retains its contents when the power is turned off, as well as 128 megabytes of much faster RAM.

It has been estimated that Google has 10 exabytes of data on disk and another five exabytes on magnetic tape.[229] And finally, various estimates of the total amount of data on the internet range from 3 to 20 or more zettabytes.[230] Now that's an overwhelming amount of data! The sheer volume of information at our fingertips, on the internet, and from other sources, is truly staggering!

carefully. We can try to interpret information we receive by comparing it to other available information, including what we have already read or heard. We can attempt to track down the pedigree of the information, the qualifications of the author or sender, and double-check key facts. We could take the journalist approach and seek two or three independent sources of the same or similar information. One of the best ways to do this is to read several articles on the same subject and to compare and judge what you believe are the "facts." This is analogous to scientists who may run several experiments to derive similar results in different ways.

It is important to remember that much of the information posted on the internet has not been double-checked for accuracy. For the most part, it has not been peer reviewed or subjected to critical evaluation by other people. Even as we hunger for online reviews of things we might want to buy or places we may want to visit, we must question the motives of the person posting each review. Is it for real? Could it be the seller or an advertiser trying to "game us"? Could it be a review paid for by the seller? Could it be "fake news" or "alternative facts"?

How can we find unbiased articles or information? We can avoid newspapers, websites, or TV networks that mainly provide one point of view, but doing so might cause us to miss a lot of useful information, which we are free to interpret in the context of other information we have. We can cast our net wider in our internet searches so we are not focusing just on policies, politics, or opinions we personally agree with. If we are reading and searching to reinforce our personal beliefs or preferences, we should be self-aware enough to recognize it and consider broadening our horizons to get a more inclusive world view.

Smart Tip

Don't believe everything you read on the internet. Look for more than one source of information about a topic and double-check important facts. Beware of opinions masquerading as facts.

Coping with Information Overload

There are several steps we can take to cope with the large amount of information we receive. We can ignore some or all of it. We can filter incoming information with "automatic" email filters based on content, or we can filter by scanning incoming information manually, focusing on the things that most interest us. We can deal with email by reading every incoming email when it arrives, just scanning titles and names on emails, or ignoring all or many of them, or anything in between.

We can take the time to sort through the incoming emails, sending selected ones to folders to save them for later action.

Smart Tip

Try not to let email rule your life. The same goes for texts and tweets! Stage a slow-down in your life for handling these kinds of real-time interruptions. Don't respond to anything quickly unless it's truly urgent. Schedule certain times of day for looking at emails and texts. Turn off your smartphone for a while, several times a day if you can, and get on with your life. Ease into these "intervention" steps, because they probably won't be easy to do.

It is often useful to be proactive and push back on junk email and spam, which makes our life easier; when in doubt, "unsubscribe." It is especially important not to "jump through the hoop" to check each email the second it comes in. The same goes for tweets and notifications and anything else that pushes itself into our lives. In general, we have to actively develop a coping strategy so we don't drown in a flood of incoming information.

We can also develop habits that prioritize how we spend our time and how much information we help "pull" in our direction so we can focus on what's most important to us with minimal interruptions. This helps us be more efficient in performing tasks because there will be fewer times we have to recover from interruptions and restart our current task.

Defer things that don't need attention right away to concentrate on tasks that are important to do now. Making to-do lists can help with prioritization and keep us from forgetting things. Overall, what we need are strategies for managing the information that we seek or that just comes our way. These strategies are very personal and revolve around our individual personality and personal preferences for getting things done.

A 2016 Pew Research Center study shows that not all Americans feel overloaded by information.[148] It concluded that people with more access to information feel less overwhelmed, showing that those people who have multiple paths to information, such as a smartphone, a smart tablet, and maybe a PC, were satisfied with the amount of information they received. Perhaps satisfaction has to do with expectations for the type and amount of incoming information. Maybe the Pew study result means that the more control we have over the information sources that we access, the better we feel about the amount of information coming our way.

It seems likely, however, that no matter what we do we are going to feel overwhelmed by all the information that we receive. We can continue to sift and sort incoming information as it comes our way. But to preserve our sanity, we should consider taking at least some steps to reduce the incoming "noise" to a dull roar.

You Can Be Overwhelmed by Technology Too

Now that we have information under control, it is time to turn

Smart Tip

Develop your own personal plan for coping with information overload. Look at approaches like avoiding or delegating tasks that involve lots of data, applying more filters to your incoming data, queueing tasks involving data so you can delay dealing with it, and ignoring some kinds of data. As you get started on your plan, you might Google "information overload," and look at several articles for ideas. You could also look for relevant books on Amazon or at a local bookstore.

to technology itself and what happens if we have too much of it. It is possible to be overwhelmed by too much technology, but the threshold depends on the person. Technology enthusiasts can't get enough of new high-tech gadgets, and they like to have them at their beck and call. Other folks may want to pick and choose the high-tech devices they want in their lives. Even if they have lots of high-tech gizmos, many people want to be alone at times without all the beeps and bonks of incoming emails and other notifications and alarms.

One reason we may feel uncomfortable with new technology is that our user interaction generally differs from device to device. Our smartphones, PCs, and smart thermostats each "speak" their own language when communicating with us, and we have to learn each one of those languages. Understanding the concept of high-tech "families" can help us learn to move more easily from device to device within each family. If you have an iPhone, you are well on your way to being able to use an iPad, which works almost the same way. The Apple family includes the iMac and MacBook, too; although their user interfaces are a little different, knowing the Apple family dialect helps you learn how to communicate with them.

People who live in the Microsoft world, with the Windows operating system, have to keep up with a somewhat different user interface, which has varied in significant ways from generation to generation of Windows. A cultural divide has developed over the years between Mac and Windows users, but there are substantial similarities in function, and if you know one interface, you can pick up the other one quickly.

TVs are similar enough that we can usually handle the remote controls and menus on a new TV, although you may sometimes need a little help. If you use one brand of TV, you can generally figure out how to turn on another brand of TV and change channels and the volume. But if you get any deeper into the functions, you may have to play around with the controls for a while or, heaven forbid, look at the instruction manual, if there is one.

Living with a gaggle of remote controls for TV, audio, and other things can sometimes be challenging. Universal remote controls can help a little bit, but they have to be set up just right to perform well, and this isn't always easy. In my family room, I have separate remote controls for a TV, an Apple TV, a Fios set-top box, a DVD player, an Amazon Fire TV Stick, a surround-sound system, and a multi-CD player. My smartphone serves as a remote for an Ecobee thermostat, the Ring doorbell, and for other things. Amazon Echos, each with Alexa, serve as remote controls for lighting and a lots of other things. We want the technology to work for us, and we understand that, at the present time, we have to put up with a lot of remote controls and different interfaces to our technology.

Too much new technology thrust upon us quickly without an opportunity to understand or assimilate it could lead to a mental block against other new technology. This would be a terrible thing, of course, since it might deter us from taking advantage of new technology that can genuinely help us in our lives. To avoid being overwhelmed, try not to buy too many new high-tech gadgets at the same time, and intentionally buy a few "retro," lower-tech devices to help balance the amount of new technology in your life.

Try to also slow down the pace of buying new high-tech devices. In general, new technology doesn't move so fast that you need the latest version of a device, so upgrading every few months, or even every year, might not be a good thing to do. There is almost always some disruption to your life when you get a new device, even one that's similar to the one you have been using. Data needs to be backed up from the device being replaced, then hopefully restored to the new device, and it may also take a while for the early bugs to be worked out with a new device through software updates or in other ways.

Smart Tip

As fun as new, high-tech gizmos are to buy and use, you may feel better about your technology if you space out your purchases rather than flood your senses and your brain with new ones all the time.

It may also be helpful to avoid developing an overdependence on any one high-tech gadget. When a high-tech device is updated, some of your favorite features might change or even be dropped from the new version. It may be better to rely on several different high-tech devices that are updated on different cycles. Many people have broken away from updating their smartphones every year or every two years, unless the hardware fails. The incremental improvements in the new versions of smartphones often appear minimal compared to the major improvements in performance and functionality in the past. If it ain't broke, don't fix it, as the saying goes!

Remember Who's in Charge!

Technology tends to surround us, to take over our work, our home, our car, our lives. To the extent we can, it is important to select technology that clearly works for us, not the other way around. We are in charge. Technology should support us and not tell us what to do.

Smart Tip

You often need to exert yourself to remain in charge of technology!

It helps to select just enough of the right technology to make our lives better. We can decide whether to buy and carry a smartphone and whether to buy a laptop or a smart tablet. We can decide whether to buy a car with all the high-tech bells and whistles or a smart TV. We can decide whether to buy a few home automation devices, then add to that if we are satisfied with them and have determined what settings best suit our preferences. We can be in charge of the technology we use most of the time by consciously making these decisions rather than just buying products willy-nilly.

We can also decide to set technology aside for a while, for

minutes or hours or longer. We can choose to turn the TV off and limit the number of hours each day it is blaring at us. We can make time to smell the roses, to savor life with our friends and everything around us, indoors and outdoors. We can be in charge of how much technology we bring into our world by putting limits on it and choosing what it does for us and when.

Use the Technology Itself to Help You

In your quest to buy and use new high-tech devices, you will sometimes need a little help to set up a device and make sure it works best for you. You may also need help when the device is not working as expected. Gone are the days of hard-copy instruction manuals; most devices come with a page or two of information at most, although a DVD with instructions is occasionally available.

When you need help, start with the technology itself. Most new high-tech devices come with built-in help functions, and most have some form of instruction manual available online. Start by clicking on the device's "help" button. You may have to look around to find it, but a help button is almost always available. You might find it in the "menu" of device options.

You can also look for the technology manufacturer's website to view questions and answers about the device or find a blog where customers share their experiences and get help from the manufacturer. A toll-free phone number is sometimes available, too. A big advantage of going online is that the advice is usually more current than hard-copy instructions. Also, searching the web using Google or Bing may result in locating the collective wisdom of people who may have similar devices and know a lot about them. Don't forget that Siri and Alexa and other high-tech helpers are standing by to listen to our questions so they can try to help us as well.

Smart Tip

Go online for help with your high-tech devices, starting with the manufacturer's website. Look for blogs and tech review sites for clues about how to use these devices, especially how to fix problems.

Simplify, Simplify, Simplify

In this complex, fast-moving world, it is helpful to take actions that simplify our lives. Simplifying is not a new thing! Here's what Leonardo da Vinci apparently had to say about it: "Simplicity is the ultimate sophistication."

We should select high-tech devices that are easy to use. And we should strive for balance in our lives between good old peace and quiet and the beeping and bonking of our smartphones, smart tablets, and other devices. We might even find time to relate to people rather than high-tech devices some of the time. So, consider surrounding yourself with fewer devices; only buy those that you really need and that you think will be fun to use.

Another way of conveying the idea of "simplicity" that resonated with my Greek father can be found in the ancient Greek saying, "everything in moderation."[149] The Greeks applied this concept to everything in life, including eating and drinking. Another way of translating this saying is "nothing in excess." This concept has also flourished in other cultures. Applied here, it means just enough technology in our lives to help us but not to distract us from living life. Don't overcomplicate life with too many high-tech devices that may take away from life itself.

Start by simplifying the process of buying high-tech

things. There is no need to make the purchasing process long and complicated. A tech buyer should take reasonable steps to select and buy things that best meet real needs. Also, don't buy too many things that may end up cluttering your life. How many high-tech things do you have sitting around, not being used? How many have you recycled or maybe even thrown out? We are tempted to keep lots of older things as we collect lots of newer things, which results in too much clutter around us. When we do this, it clutters our mind and makes it difficult to focus on what we are doing. Too many high-tech gizmos sitting around makes our high-tech world feel more complex and harder to live with. By refraining from buying things you don't really need, you are likely to feel better about the things you do buy.

Once you have bought your new high-tech devices, enjoy them and show them off. Determine which features of each device you are going to make a regular part of your life. If you are like me, you probably won't use half the features of each new device you buy. Don't worry about it. You will gradually find that some of the features you aren't using may be useful after all, perhaps after you have read an article that discusses them.

Smart Tip

Simplify your life by only using the features in your devices that you really need and are comfortable using. You may find some of the other features useful later, but you can ignore them for now.

You could say that this advice is just applying the old KISS Principle (Keep It Simple Stupid) that many of us have heard from time to time. Well, this principle is alive and well in the world of new technology. It applies to the people who design and build new devices as well as to device users. For example, maybe we shouldn't automatically buy or activate all the bells and whistles on a smartphone, PC, or even a car, if we don't need them.

Remember, these nice-to-haves introduce complexity. If we are to maintain some degree of control over our lives, including how we interact with technological devices, then the simpler the devices are, the better off we are. This simplicity will put us in a better position to exert control over the technology instead of being overwhelmed by it. We can't be in charge if things are so complicated that we never become fully aware about how to use them well.

New technology can look deceivingly simple because the complex details are often disguised by a well-designed user interface, which can be good thing. The look and feel of new technology is not just a question of style; Apple vs. Microsoft, for example. The user interface is a way to make new things more accessible and appealing. Steve Jobs and his design partner Jonathan Ive, who was Apple's chief design officer for years, were onto something important when they brought us high-tech devices that look and feel good, work smoothly, and are remarkably simple to use.

Steve Jobs said that "simple can be harder than complex: You have to work hard to get your thinking clean to make it simple. But it's worth it in the end because once you get there, you can move mountains."[150] This is, of course, consistent with the Apple approach toward designing very complex things to make them easy and straightforward to use. The underlying complexity has been hidden in a particularly effective way.

However, you should recognize that a complex device that is made to look simple may be an illusion. It may be taking control from you and doing things its way, the way it is programmed to do or maybe even the way it has learned to do. It may be deceiving you by not letting you know what is really going on because it looks so simple to use. Beware the conniving high-tech gadget that is designed to look simple but may be taking over your life. Yes, this is an exaggeration. You should be targeting "real" simplicity in your life, even when high-tech gizmos may be conspiring to make your life complex. Just turn off some of the features that make these things become so complex, and don't be afraid to turn the offending devices themselves off for a while. That will tell them who is in charge! And that will make your new, simplified life more peaceful and enjoyable.

Smart Tip

Consider introducing some retro things into your life to simplify your world, even if you just buy a few old fashioned analog clocks. A few low-tech things may help us become more comfortable with the high-tech things we depend on, helping us relax more and not feel pressured by the face of technology every moment of the day. In coffee shops or other public spaces, don't spend all your time staring at a smartphone or a laptop! You can even chat with other people! Changing some things around you so they don't go beep or bonk can be an important part of your new simplifying mantra.

Simplify by Going Back in Time

Some people are simplifying their lives by moving back to typewriters and away from PCs, smart tablets, and smartphones. Some seasoned writers rely on typewriters as their "old friends" and view them as partners in their work. Aspiring writers sometimes use typewriters in hopes of replicating the styles of earlier authors. *Times of London* set up a speaker in the newsroom that played typewriter sounds to boost staff energy levels.[231] Some governments are considering using typewriters to reduce the risk of cyberattacks.[232] Typewriters are still sold on Amazon and in stores as well.

So, if you simplify and simplify some more, while making sure you are still in charge, you will enjoy all your new technology more.

The theme in this chapter is to prevent technology from intruding too much in your life. This thought is especially appropriate considering how mesmerizing our new, high-tech devices can be. We can easily be entranced by the things these devices do for us and the way they do them because they are so "cool." Cool is just fine, but don't get too carried away. Now that you are in good shape to tame the high-tech beast, the next chapter will give you a glimpse into the future, which will bring high-tech gizmos that are even more fun!

Key Points

- All day long we are subjected to a barrage of information. Emails and texts, websites we visit for news and social networking. We can help reduce the information overload that we face every day by developing our own personal plan for coping with information overload.
- We have all learned, sometimes the hard way, that what we see on the internet may not be real or true. Beware of opinions masquerading as facts, look for more than one source of information about a topic, and double-check important facts.
- It is possible to be overwhelmed by too much information or technology, but the threshold for this depends on the individual.
- You often need to exert yourself to remain in charge of technology. Don't update your technology too often, and don't buy more than you need.
- Use the technology's built-in help tools when you get stuck, and don't be afraid to ask for assistance when you need it.
- In this complex, fast-moving world, it's important to simplify our high-tech lives.

CHAPTER 10

WHAT'S IN OUR FUTURE?

WE NOW ARE PREPARED to survive the new technology that we already have or will soon buy and enjoy. But the march of new technology will continue at a fast pace, and we need to be ready for it. Predicting the future is quite difficult, especially when trying to predict revolutionary changes. Even predicting evolutionary change is hard, but it's much easier using recent past trends as a guide. This chapter focuses on likely evolutionary changes. Where is technology headed, and what does that mean for us?

Expect Even More New Technology

While it might be hard to imagine since we already live in a technology-enabled world, there will be much more technology in our future. So what will be different with technology over the next several years? We will have self-driving cars, even smarter smart things working for us, faster high-tech devices that are more responsive, and more capable voice-driven virtual assistants. We will have a real partnership with our high-tech devices — our tech assistants.

Our tech assistants will be at our service, helping and serving us, all day and all night. Beginning when we wake up in the morning, they will know our schedule for the day and make sure we are prepared for everything we and others have planned. We will wake up at the right time, coordinated with our sleep pattern, so we feel fresh and ready to go. Based on our calendar for the day, and considering the weather and the traffic, our wakeup helper will decide when to gently awaken us. We will have had a great night's sleep, because the house-minder assistant will have heated or cooled the house perfectly, so everyone is comfortable, and it will have minded the house while were asleep, securing everything and watching for anything that needs special attention. It will automatically take care of things around the house and alert us if something needs our personal intervention.

After we awake, we will be reminded of what we have planned for the day, including anything that has been added to our schedule by others. We will be coached if we need to wear something special for a big meeting or other event during the day. A little soothing or energy-boosting music will help us adjust to being awake, based on what our high-tech helpers know about our preferred early morning music.

As we get dressed and prepare to take on the world, we will be brought up to date on the latest news and weather, with an emphasis on information that is most relevant to our plans for the day. And, yes, the coffee will be ready when we are, either at home or at our nearby Starbucks. Our high-tech assistants will have coordinated our family's activities, too, making time for us to be together for a while, if possible, and helping everyone get ready for work and school. Each person in the household will have their own personal, high-tech assistant, and the assistants will all work together.

All day long, our incoming emails and texts will be responded to automatically, based on our preferences, to the extent the email assistant is able to do so. Our friends and colleagues probably won't notice that we haven't responded personally. That's how good the AI-based high-tech assistants will be, and our tech assistant will learn from experience every day, too, so it will perform better over time.

If we are driving, our car navigation system will be preprogrammed by our personal tech assistant to help us with the day's schedule. The car may even be one that drives itself, either completely autonomously or with a little help from us. On-call car-sharing services, accessed through smartphones, will be viable alternatives to owning and driving our own cars, even more than they are today.

Self-Driving Cars Are Just Around the Corner

Almost every day there is an announcement of still more functionality planned for future cars. We are moving in the direction of self-driving cars, although truly autonomous or driverless cars are still several years away. The terminology used for cars that "almost" self-drive varies depending on the manufacturer and how brazen their advertising is. Tech-assisted driving is made possible by radar in the front and, sometimes, in the back of our cars; lidar sensors; video cameras; ultrasonic sensors; and onboard computers that model the environment around the car. Google has had self-driving cars on the road in "test mode" since about 2012, with over 2 million miles of test driving.[151]

Key Word

Lidar is "light detection and ranging" — essentially light radar that makes images of objects and determines their distance from us.

Several brands of cars now include assisted driving technology that takes them part way toward self-driving.[152] Key driving features necessary to have this capability are stop-and-go adaptive cruise control (ACC) and automated, lane-centering steering. Lots of cars have ACC with stop-and-go, and many brands have "lane-keeping assist," which helps a car keep away from the lines at the edge of the driving lane. But few brands have full, lane-centered steering, and only a few of these have lane-centering that works well, meaning they follow marked lanes having mild turns, on limited access roads, and, in some cases, on selected specially mapped highways. These brands, according to early 2019 reporting, are Tesla and General Motors Cadillac. Tesla calls its system Autopilot, and the system on the Cadillac CT6 is called GM Super Cruise.

Tesla's Autopilot enables a car to follow other cars and keep in lane. The technology also includes automatic parking, a way to "summon" your parked car, and automated lane change after the driver has hit the turn signal lever.[153] Tesla has been improving its cars' ability to perform more driving tasks without human help by using its large database of Tesla driving experience. The company taps this database to compare real drivers with what Autopilot would have done.[154] Tesla can do this because all its cars send lots of data back to the company when they are on the road, even when the cars are being driven by humans.

Ride-sharing companies Uber and Lyft are moving aggressively toward self-driving vehicles as well, with the goal being autonomous vehicle fleets. John Zimmer, co-founder of Lyft, predicted in 2016 that within five years most Lyft rides will be in self-driving cars.[155] Waymo, the self-driving car subsidiary of Alphabet (parent company of Google), continues its extensive technology development through its Waymo One self-driving taxi service.[156] This service operates in Phoenix, Arizona,

Key Words

Adaptive cruise control is a system that enables a car to follow the one in front of it, speeding up and slowing down as necessary, sometimes coming to a complete stop and starting up again, as in stop-and-go traffic. **Automated lane-centering steering** keeps your car in its lane using a camera that visually looks at lane markings on the road.

providing paid service to selected customers who provide feedback on their experiences. Waymo One cars reportedly have a safety driver, and the driver has to take over occasionally, such as when it rains or if the taxi gets confused by a left turn.

Self-driving trucks are also being tested and could be on the road soon. Proponents say that robot trucks will be much safer because machines don't get tired, distracted, drink alcohol, or take drugs. Just like with car drivers, errors by truck drivers account for 90 percent of truck accidents.

Although news reports of accidents involving self-driving or partially self-driving cars get a lot of attention, statistics indicate that self-driving cars have the potential to reduce auto fatalities.[157] More than 30,000 lives are lost each year in traffic accidents in the US and there are 1.2 million fatalities globally. Some researchers estimate fatalities could be reduced by up to 90 percent with cars driving themselves.[158]

Self-Driving Cars Still Have a Lot to "Learn"

Although self-driving cars are poised to gain in popularity, there are still challenges that need to be overcome. For example, these cars must be able to successfully navigate road construction, including understanding hand gestures by construction workers, which can lead to chaotic road conditions that are hard to predict.[159] Snow and ice and low visibility on roads also pose challenges, as do pedestrians, bicycles, and children playing near the street.

"Who's at fault" could be a critical consideration in the introduction of self-driving cars. Even with widely used advanced driver assist capabilities like adaptive cruise control, some people may blame the car and its manufacturer if the car doesn't execute assistive functions correctly or as the driver believed they would be executed, and this contributed to an accident. Teslas that were on Autopilot have been involved in accidents, such as highway crashes near Washington, DC, and Los Angeles, in which the Tesla didn't "see" a stopped car on the highway ahead, and the drivers weren't able to avoid a collision.[160] Fortunately, the drivers weren't seriously injured. However, there was another accident in Florida in which a Tesla on Autopilot slammed into a large truck that had moved across the highway in front of the car.[161] Neither the Autopilot nor the driver saw the truck, and the driver was killed. Tesla and other companies are working to improve self-driving software that senses and takes appropriate action in these types of situations, including improved performance when driving directly into glaring sunlight and in winter weather.

The Problem with Humans

One dilemma facing automakers as they introduce more and more self-driving technology is that drivers are being forced to give up key aspects of the "feel" of driving the car, according to the *Washington Post*.[162] Features like adaptive cruise control and automatic steering threaten the driver's "freedom, independence, and control of the road." The *Washington Post* article reports that "carmakers increasingly are selling the illusion of control, while, in practice, taking more and more away." A 2018 Autotrader survey reports that Americans do not want to cede control of their car, with 84 percent wanting the option to drive themselves, even in a self-driving car.[163] But, at the same time, they are willing to pay for the car features that take control away from them.

Another concern is that self-driving cars tested on the road so far have been literally "following all the rules," such as driving no faster than the speed limit.[164] Google learned that the cars are "a little more cautious than they need to be," according to Chris Urmson, former CTO of Google's self-driving car team and now CEO of Aurora, a self-driving car start-up company. He also said that "we are trying to make them drive more humanistically."[165] Human drivers seldom follow all the rules of the road, so when another car does so, it can frustrate them. This has apparently led to accidents, such as self-driving cars being rear-ended when they come to a full stop in unexpected places. So, we need to "train" self-driving cars not to drive quite so carefully, to cut corners, edge into intersections, and sometimes even cross double center lines, just like humans do.[166] Also, different states and cities have different driving cultures, and self-driving cars need to adapt to them. For example, Pittsburgh is reported to have an unwritten left-turn rule that allows the first car turning left at an intersection to do so in front of cars coming straight across in the other direction.[167]

Stay Tuned for Self-Driving Cars . . . Sometime

Concern has been expressed by many knowledgeable people that we still have a very long way to go to have truly "driverless cars," according to a 2017 article in *Science Magazine*.[168] The article's author, Jeffrey Mervis, concludes that most transportation experts say truly autonomous driving is still decades away. Many people think driverless cars will help in some ways, while also adding to the world's pressing problems because more reliance on cars will result in increased congestion, energy consumption, and air pollution.

There have been many optimistic claims made by developers of self-driving cars, combined with unclear definitions of terms like "autonomous vehicles." There is healthy skepticism about Tesla's claims that it will have full self-driving cars soon, and some studies have shown other companies have self-driving cars equal or ahead of Tesla technology.[169] The CEO of Waymo, John Krafcik, predicted in early 2019 that 2030 would be a good "target date" for the introduction of fully functional autonomous vehicles, true self-driving cars.[170] European Union commissioner for transport, Violeta Bulc, has also identified 2030 as the likely year for a "new generation of vehicles that will be fully automated."[171]

There has been insufficient attention to the difficult problem of humans monitoring a self-driving car's performance, but not being able to take action quickly enough if they are needed. (See the "We Will Be Real Partners with Technology" section, later in this chapter, for more about this.) I predict it may take years for manufacturers to solve these kinds of problems. Meanwhile, government officials will be deciding when it is safe enough to allow driverless cars on the road, knowing that they are likely to be involved in some accidents, including ones with injuries or fatalities.

Technology Will Be Smarter and Smarter

By some measures and predictions, computers that employ AI are beginning to look like they are intelligent. Noted technology innovator and forecaster Ray Kurzweil predicted in 2009 that by about 2019 computers costing about $4,000 will have the power of a human brain.[172] That prediction turned out to be pretty accurate, although there is no agreed-on measure of the power of the human brain. Kurzweil also predicted the onset of the "Singularity" by 2045—when computers are so smart that civilization will be profoundly changed. Well-known scientist and former MIT president Jerome Weisner once said, "We can always pull the plug," which might be necessary if Kurzweil is correct! The Singularity is sometimes referred to as the true beginning of artificial general intelligence.[173] Intelligence has been defined in a number of ways, such as a person's capacity for logic or abstract thought, understanding, and problem-solving, and the ability to acquire, understand, and use knowledge.[174] General intelligence is what is typically measured when someone takes an IQ test.

In a 2015 article in the *Washington Post*, technology entrepreneur and university professor Vivek Wadhwa referenced Moore's Law (See "Even Faster and Cheaper Tech in the Palm of Our Hand," later in this chapter) and Kurzweil's predictions, together with the observed progression of iPhones, and predicted that "within seven years [of 2015] the smartphones in our pockets will be as computationally intelligent as we are."[175] More recently, there have been predictions that specialized chips, such as "deep neural AI" chips, will be included in smartphones, giving them high-performance capabilities for sophisticated tasks without having to connect to the cloud.[176] My iPhone 8 has a "neural engine," which Apple says helps the smartphone recognize faces better.

One of the most visible recent implementations of AI technology is IBM's Watson, which uses deep learning and other AI techniques.[177] Deep learning, which is the use of deep artificial neural networks, has proved to be very effective for solving problems within specific knowledge areas, such as helping doctors diagnose illnesses and develop treatment options. In its public debut, Watson used natural language processing, together with statistical analysis of a large numbers of documents containing words, to determine likely answers to "Jeopardy!" questions — and it won in grand style.

IBM has developed a commercial version of Watson by teaming with NVIDIA, a company that creates powerful

For the Tech Curious

Artificial neural networks are computing systems inspired by the biological neural networks in the human brain. The neurons are structured like the brain's neurons and interconnected like the brain's neural network. Each neuron has several "inputs" and, usually, one "output." The output is determined by the neuron's input signals. Each of the inputs is assigned a different "weight" as they are combined to produce the neuron's output. A weight of two for one input and one for another means that the first input is twice as influential in determining the output.

Training artificial neural networks is an iterative process. Networks are trained to learn new tasks by applying thousands of examples of inputs and outputs, then adjusting and refining the weights of the inputs at each step to produce the desired outputs. Artificial neural networks can be trained to solve complex problems, such as detecting credit card fraud, autofocusing a camera, and recognizing faces.[233]

Artificial neural networks are usually layered, with the outputs of one layer comprising the inputs of the next layer. Deep neural networks are generally defined as having four or more layers of neurons, enabling them to perform better than neural networks with only two or three layers.

Key Word

Natural language processing is a computer's interpretation of words spoken or written in English or another natural language. The computer uses its interpretation to determine meaning so action can be taken responding to the words.

graphics processing units (GPUs) for high-end graphic-display workstations and some of the fastest supercomputers in the world. The commercial version of Watson provides high-performance, deep-learning applications and is sold as a cloud-based service. IBM also offers hardware and software for building your own Watson.[178] Among the widely publicized applications is H&R Block's use of Watson to provide improved tax preparation services, but that seems like overkill for most people.[179]

AI enthusiasts have always been overly optimistic when forecasting significant improvement in AI capability. It is one thing for a computer to "appear to be" smart in specific knowledge areas by human standards. It is another thing for a computer to be able to understand and solve problems in a wide range of subject areas or knowledge domains. Humans sometimes assume that because a computer can solve specific problems so well and so fast that it can accomplish similar feats across many areas of knowledge.

Early AI has been focused on limited domains of knowledge, like playing checkers or chess or understanding numbers spoken by humans. A computer can seem smart because it is so fast at calculating or looking things up, as well as using specialized tools like artificial neural networks, but it is really just doing a lot of simple things very quickly. That said, the results of applying AI today to specific problems are generally far better than they were a decade or two ago.

An Important AI Application: Voice Recognition

Similarly, when high-tech devices, such as Amazon's Echo with Alexa and Apple's Siri, appear to understand our spoken words and speak back to us, we get the impression that the devices are smart. The speech recognition of these "assistants" is getting better and better, usually using AI techniques, and the quality of their computer-generated responses is improving as well. Although we think of these assistants as right next to us, available instantly when we say their name or push a button, almost all their functions, including voice recognition, are largely implemented out in the cloud, connected to us through our iPhone or Amazon Echo.

Evidence that speech recognition has come a long way in recent years is illustrated by a 2015 *USA Today* report stating that Google had at that time reduced word-error rates to about 8 percent, compared to around 25 percent a few years earlier.[180] That article also notes that "some of the improvement can be traced to advances in computing power, machine learning techniques, and natural language processing." Google reports that its speech recognition capability can accommodate speakers using 58 languages.

Efforts are well underway to develop new capabilities for smartphones and other consumer electronics that will further improve their understanding of speech, as well as their ability to process images from cameras by incorporating advanced AI hardware and software, such as deep neural network processors.[181] The neural networks in these processors still need to be trained using lots of data. But the trained neural networks can be loaded into the memory of these devices before they are delivered to users. As improved software and supporting data, including improved neural networks, become available for smartphones and other high-tech devices, they can be downloaded as software updates.

Although voice-responding high-tech assistants will continue to gain new capabilities, their limitations still include an inability to comprehend a wide range of requests and to remember one part of a conversation with a user so it can be used when responding to subsequent questions and requests. Most of the progress we have witnessed from these products is the result of receiving a lot of help from cloud-based computing to perform many functions. As powerful as the computers are in smartphones, it is not enough to provide serious voice-response and AI-based response handling without lots of support from cloud-based computers. When smartphones and similar devices are disconnected from their cloud tether, they are generally only able to communicate with us in a much more limited way. In the future, when trained neural networks can be incorporated into these devices, they will be able to do much more without having to connect to the cloud.

We now expect voice recognition to work very well and have been responding by voice rather than keypad for over a decade when navigating telephone menus for large companies. Voice recognition systems in cars generally work quite well, too, but drivers usually have to conform their commands to what the navigation system can handle. Some speech recognition systems work better after they are trained to respond to the user's voice, a capability that some cars have. My car's navigation system can listen to my voice and perform a Google search to look up an "online destination." It then downloads the destination's coordinates and sets up the navigation system to direct my car there. It's quite impressive in action.

Smarter Than We Are?

A number of bright and knowledgeable people are concerned that AI could eventually spell doom for humankind by leading to technology that is "too smart." Ray Kurzweil, the noted technologist and futurist who has predicted that computers will soon be as smart as humans, argues that "technology always has been a double-edged sword, since fire kept us warm but also burned down our villages."

In a talk at MIT in 2014 as reported by the *Washington Post*, Elon Musk, of Tesla and SpaceX fame, said, "I think we should be careful about artificial intelligence. If I were to guess what our biggest existential threat is, it's probably that."[182] CBS News has reported that Musk has also said, "We need to be super careful with AI. [It is] potentially more dangerous than nukes."[183]

The late Stephen Hawking, who was a famous and incredibly smart cosmologist, issued a warning to humankind about artificial intelligence. As reported by the *Washington Post*, he said "I think the development of full artificial intelligence could spell the end of the human race."[184] According to an article on the Geek website, Hawking said in 2015 that "computers will overtake humans with AI sometime within the next 100 years. When that happens, we need to make sure the computers have [their] goals aligned with ours."[185]

Steve Wozniak, co-founder of Apple and designer of the Apple I and the Apple II, has been quoted as saying that "computers are going to take over from humans, no question."[186]

The *Washington Post* reported that Microsoft founder Bill Gates has joined the crowd warning about the dangers of AI. He said, "I am in the camp that is concerned about super intelligence. First the machines will do a lot of jobs for us and not be super intelligent. That should be positive if we manage it well. A few decades after that, though, the intelligence is strong enough to be a concern."[187]

However, in *The Glass Cage*, author Nicholas Carr quotes the famous British mathematician and computer scientist Alan M. Turing, who asserted that "we need not worry that computers, with their algorithmic processes, will replace human intuition or human 'spontaneous judgments.'"[188] Humans draw from a wealth of personal experience and education when they make decisions, and we have an amazing ability to conceptualize and apply knowledge across specific knowledge domains that computers are quite unlikely to replicate or simulate any time soon.

I believe we need not worry too much because AI has been moving forward in fits and starts for the last 50 years, and we still have only "limited domain" AI applications. For example, we have AI applications that can sometimes pick faces out of the crowd and help doctors analyze enzymes to determine whether someone is having a heart attack. It is hard to conceive of building a machine in the foreseeable future that will have generalized AI of the kind that has been of concern to super smart people like Hawking, Gates, Wozniak, and Kurzweil, but we need to be cautious over the long term as this kind of technology becomes more powerful.

We Will Be Partners with Our Technology

Rather than relying on AI to help our high-tech devices get smarter and smarter, we can partner with technology to do much more—and do it better—than either people or machines can do by themselves.

One way of being real partners with technology was first proposed by J.C.R. Licklider, MIT professor and a leader of ARPA, the US Department of Defense agency that developed the ARPANET (see more about him in Chapter 5). In 1960, he stated in a historically important paper that "the hope is that human brains and computing machines will be coupled together very tightly, and that the resulting partnership will think as no human brain has ever thought and process data in a way not approached by the information-handling machines we know today."[189]

I was so impressed by Licklider and his vision for a complementary, symbiotic relationship between man and machine that in 1968 I wrote in the book *Advances in Computers, Volume 8*, "if the successful interaction of man and machine furthers the relegation of man to an insignificant position, it must be regarded with extreme caution. If, however, this symbiosis can be made to assist man to fulfill his greatest potential, then it must be vigorously pursued."[190]

Licklider's vision influenced some of the key people who built early hypertext systems and even the World Wide Web. He inspired the late Doug Engelbart, who was a highly regarded computer science researcher. Engelbart also developed very capable computer-based tools, like the Augmenting the Human Intellect (AHI) concept, to help humans work smarter. The goal of this concept was to augment a human's ability to solve complex tasks and handle information through collaboration with machines. I remember how excited I was when Doug demonstrated his online system (known as NLS) and let me try it. NLS supported collaboration, hypertext links, windowing, and other new concepts, and, of course, used a mouse, which Engelbart had invented![191] I felt a partnership with the system he had built, and it left a lasting impression. Many of his ideas were incorporated in later research at the Xerox Palo Alto Research Center (PARC) that led to the personal computing technology we take for granted today. See Chapter 5 for more information about Xerox PARC.

More recently, the IBM teams that built Watson and Deep Blue (a chess-playing computer that won a game against a world-champion chess player) adopted a symbiotic approach, rather than focusing on a set of AI tools that did all the work without human help. John Kelly III, director of IBM Research, has said "this isn't about replacing human thinking with machine thinking. Rather, in the era of cognitive systems, humans and machines will collaborate to produce better results, each bringing their own superior skills to the partnership."[192]

Chess grandmaster Garry Kasparov, after his loss to Deep Blue, set up an experiment in which he demonstrated that two American chess amateurs who partnered with three computers could do very well. He said, "Their skill at manipulating and coaching their computers to look very deeply into positions effectively counteracted the superior chess understanding of their grandmaster opponents and the greater computational power of other participants."[193]

American writer and journalist Walter Isaacson has speculated that "no matter how fast computers progress, artificial intelligence may never outstrip the intelligence of the human-machine partnership."[194] He says that "artificial intelligence need not be the holy grail of computing. The goal instead could be to find ways to optimize the collaboration between human and machine capabilities—to forge a partnership in which we let the machines do what they do best, and they let us do what we do best."

Applying this concept to self-driving cars, we may need to keep humans in control at least some of the time under routine driving conditions if we ever expect them to take action when the automated systems fail or run into conditions they can't handle. It can take up to 15 or more seconds for a human driver to observe road conditions and determine what action is necessary before they can be in a position to take over, depending on what the driver was doing when the car asked the driver to take over.[195]

In the book *Our Robots, Ourselves*: *Robotics and the Myths of Autonomy*, David Mindell envisions a future in which humans are kept in the loop, for many good reasons, rather than relegated to being passengers or observers in automated cars or other high-tech autonomous devices.[196] Collaboration with technology—being partners with our "almost" self-driving cars, smartphones, and other advanced technology—can offer the best balance of humans and machines working together to accomplish many tasks.

Vastly Improved Voice-Driven Virtual Assistants

The high-tech assistants that listen to what we say and take actions based on our words will become much smarter over the next several years. We may not see these assistants, but we sometimes see the smart speakers, the physical devices that contain the microphones and speakers for them.[197] Sometimes, the smart speakers are hidden inside things like smart thermostats or wall switches. The entity that listens and responds to our questions or requests can be called a "virtual assistant." It isn't a physical assistant, although some of the electronic logic that makes it work is in the speaker/microphone box or the iPhone.

As enablers for future virtual assistants, voice recognition and natural language processing will get even smarter over the next decade or two as they take advantage of improved AI and large databases. When voice recognition is combined with a capability to take actions or respond using a synthesized human voice, things start to get interesting. It's the connection to large databases in the cloud that enables voice-driven assistants to answer questions. It is the network connectivity to things around us, such as thermostats, home lighting, sound systems, and car navigation systems, that makes voice assistants so powerful and enables them to help us in many ways.

We are on the verge of telling everything around us what

to do by talking to a voice-driven assistant, which then tells the things around us what to do. Siri has been on iPhones for several years and is used by over 300 million people.[198] Apple has included Siri in its HomePod speaker, too. Amazon's Alexa, which is now embedded in over 30 million Amazon Echo and Dot smart speakers, as well as devices from other manufacturers, such as Sonos wireless speakers, can be used to control many other devices. For example, Alexa can control an Ecobee thermostat and lights and locks that are connected to a Wink hub.[199] A hub, you may recall from "The Things Are Coming!", Chapter 8, connects different devices in the home or elsewhere, translating the "protocols" or language used by each device, so other devices understand.

Alexa listens to us and can initiate over 25,000 "skills," such as play music, answer questions, buy things on Amazon, send email and texts, and adjust a thermostat. Similarly, Google Assistant answers questions, finds directions, sends email, and takes many other actions. Google Home is a smart speaker that essentially includes Google Assistant and is comparable to the Amazon Echo. Microsoft has added functionality to its Cortana virtual assistant so it does more than help Windows' desktop users. It can play music, speak reminders, provide a weather report, and much more.[200]

Voice-driven assistants represent a highly competitive market, with developers trying to differentiate their products. Voice recognition technology, combined with natural language processing to interpret the structure of the sentences being spoken, is maturing well. But the things that can be done with voice input are still limited, even with real-time access to substantial supporting resources in the cloud. In addition, there is increasing concern about these devices capturing conversations not intended for them, including accidentally triggering an extended recording and even sending the "eavesdropped" conversation to people who should not hear it. This happens in part as a result of efforts to make the devices more sensitive, ready to respond even if the wake-up word, such as "Alexa," is spoken softly or from a distance or by someone with an unfamiliar accent.[201] These devices can sometimes make users vulnerable to improper or unauthorized use of the recorded audio by the manufacturers of the devices and others.

The *Wall Street Journal* reported that in May 2018 an Amazon Echo device mistakenly recorded a private conversation and sent it to someone on the owner's contact list. Amazon later stated that the device misunderstood pieces of the conversation as commands that led to an extended recording and delivery of it to an unintended recipient.[202] The *Wall Street Journal* provides some tips on keeping these types of devices as secure as possible, including changing the default settings, not buying them secondhand after they were set up and used by another person, and restricting functions, such as shopping, so they can be used by only one voice or person. Obviously, it may be in your best interest to restrict what you say when in hearing range of these devices or to turn them off if you want old fashioned privacy. Of course, you won't have to worry

Smart Tip

Consider limiting voice shopping using a smart speaker to someone who has a preset "confirmation code" so your children or others don't order things they want — leaving you with the bill. You can establish this limitation through the device settings.

Careful What You Say

Check the privacy settings for your voice-driven personal assistant and pay close attention to what is being recorded "forever." Most voice assistants function with support from computer servers in the cloud. Make sure you understand your privacy options, if any. The computers in the cloud record what has been said to the voice assistant, sometimes even when you don't realize they are recording, like when the device "thinks" it heard its name being called when we didn't intentionally do so. Generally, the recordings of everything that has ever been said to the voice assistant are kept "forever," unless you are proactive to delete some or all of them.

Transcripts of what has been said to the voice assistants are usually stored, and you may have to do a lot of searching to determine what the policies are for your voice assistant and how to delete these recordings. Sometimes, you can only delete the recordings one by one, and it can take a long time to delete hundreds or thousands of such recordings. Amazon says you can never delete their transcripts of your Alexa voice recordings![234]

about these issues if you don't buy and use a voice-driven virtual assistant, but you also will miss out on all the things it can do for you.

Over the next decade, we are going to be living in a world in which we will be surrounded by microphones and cameras. In our homes and our cars we should be able to place some constraints on when and how we are being listened to and watched. We can choose to turn microphones off or not buy devices that have microphones. We can turn off cameras or tape over their lenses. We can leave some of the microphones on and rely on a voice recognition system to recognize when we are speaking to them by saying their wakeup keyword, like "Alexa."

When we are relying on a device to detect our spoken keyword, we should understand that what we say after the keyword will be recorded, along with a half second or more of what we said before the keyword is spoken. The digital recording of our voice is likely to be sent, for interpretation and to initiate actions, through the internet to the company that developed the device. The recording is likely to be stored in the cloud, perhaps for years, to help improve the long-term performance of the device or for other purposes. Alternatively, some devices can be set to require that a button be pressed to activate voice recognition, as I do with Siri on my iPhone, and as many of us do to when speaking to our car navigation systems.

You Haven't Seen Anything Yet

We can expect that voice assistants will expand their areas of expertise over the next several years, and these tools will become so good that we will become dependent on them, rather than treat them as a curiosity. We will be able to carry on a conversation with these devices, too, as they become able to respond conversationally to a series of recent requests, instead of just responding to individual queries one at a time.

These improved capabilities will rely on larger, better databases that provide access to information in multiple knowledge domains. Voice assistants will also have additional short-term memory for each user, so they can effectively respond in the context of the user's recent requests. The logic used to answer questions and to respond to requests for action will be more sophisticated and will be aided by AI. Voice assistants will be by our side all the time—at home, at the office, in our cars, in our pockets, and, in the distant future, probably attached to or embedded in our bodies!

Faster and Cheaper Tech in the Palm of Our Hand

Electronic devices, the heart and soul of new technology, will continue to get faster and faster. A primary driving force toward faster electronic devices is known as Moore's Law, which observes that, over time, more and more components will fit on a semiconductor chip. This law is the rule of thumb which has been leading to increased chip density that results in more capability and higher performance. In 1965, Intel's Gordon Moore formulated Moore's Law, which projected that the number of transistors on a chip would increase by 200 percent a year.[203] The law was later reformulated by David House, Moore's Intel colleague, who "factored in the increasing performance of transistors, to conclude that integrated circuits would double in performance every 18 months."[204] The law is sometimes interpreted expansively, as the driver for reducing costs and improving the performance of everything electronic.

I have experienced Moore's Law firsthand through a progression of PCs I have owned. My first home PC was an original IBM PC, with an Intel 8086 processor. This processor contained 29,000 transistors.[205] The processor in the Dell PC I am using to write this book is an Intel Core i7-4790, which was introduced in 2014 and contains 1.4 billion transistors. This processor is a lot faster, too, and my current PC costs less than the early IBM PC. When I use this PC as a word processor, as I am doing this very moment, it is no faster at the word processing task than the early PC, but the word processing software (Word 2013) has a lot more functionality. Now, the document being created is displayed on the screen looking very much like it will when it is printed, a capability known as What You See is What You Get (WYSIWYG). You may recall from Chapter 5 that this was a revolutionary development that came out of Xerox PARC in 1977.[206]

By 2015, the doubling of the number of transistors on a

chip had begun stretching out to every 24 months, and it has been predicted by 2020 to be every 36 months. This is a result of technological limits on how small things can be fabricated on a chip. Although there may still be some late-life extenders for Moore's Law, we won't have the benefit of it forever. We have been spoiled by modern-day electronic devices as their design, manufacture, and performance have followed Moore's Law. Each new generation of TV, PC, laptop, smartphone, and their brethren is better and cheaper. We are reaching the point where the components on chips are approaching atomic scale, so small that each component will soon be composed of just a few atoms. But the fast-approaching death of Moore's Law is spurring innovation that will enable us to continue being spoiled by the rapid introduction of new kinds of electronic technology.[207]

One of the ways to continue providing better performance without the benefit of Moore's Law is the trend toward parallelism on the semiconductor chip level as well in overall computer architecture.[208] Using multiple processors working together, rather than just one, has the potential to speed up work, if the processors can be successfully managed. This parallelism trend has helped overcome the speed and associated heat dissipation limitations of silicon-based integrated circuits. Since it is becoming impractical to make individual processors faster, two, four, or eight processors can be placed on a single microprocessor chip. The microprocessor in my current PC is quad-core, which means it has four processors. The challenge with this approach is being able to program the multiprocessor system to take advantage of the parallelism and to obtain reasonable efficiency in the use of the processor hardware.

Parallel computing has been around for years in the largest and fastest supercomputers, and programming them has been an art that has become well-developed over the last several decades. This has enabled the supercomputer field to move to what is sometimes called "massively parallel computing," where thousands of processor chips, each of which may have four, eight, or 16 or more processors, are used in one supercomputer. Now, some of the parallel programming techniques developed for supercomputers are being used in PCs and smartphones.

Another trend to increase the performance of PCs, smartphones, and other smart devices is the use of specialized processors to augment general-purpose processors. This began by using graphics processing unit (GPU) technology, (originally developed for video gaming) working in tandem with "ordinary" processors to increase overall performance. The development of multicore integrated circuits that have one or more traditional processors, a GPU, and other specialized processors, provides some breathing room as Moore's Law can no longer be relied on for long-term performance gains.

One example of the progress being made using this technology is the Apple A11 Bionic processor chip, which is in the iPhone 8, 8 Plus, and the iPhone X. The A11 chip was introduced in 2017 and contains 4.3 billion transistors.[209] The A11 includes a fast GPU and a motion coprocessor, as well as an image processor and a neural engine that implements machine learning algorithms to accelerate image recognition, such as when using Face ID. The chip includes six general-purpose processors, two of which are high performance and four of which are slower but said to be energy-efficient.[210] With all this capability and more in the palm of our hand, our expectations for higher speed and improved capability can continue rising rather than stagnating as it would if we were to continue to rely only on Moore's Law.

Will We Ever Be Alone Again?

While all these technological developments are very exciting, this march of technology can seem overwhelming for some of us. If we begin to feel like it's too much for us, can we take a technology time-out? Sometimes we can. But we may feel the peer pressure of our friends and encouragement to buy from companies that develop and sell new technology. And, as we've seen, high-tech devices may be listening to us or watching us, giving us little opportunity to be alone, even for a little while.

We sometimes face insistent "push" technology that sends alerts as unsolicited texts or emails to us. Push vs. pull is a basic concept in the design of human-computer interfaces. Pushing allows devices to interrupt us with an alert that something has happened or the device just wants our attention. Pulling forces devices to wait for us to ask for something before sending it, such as when we ask a question and expect an answer. Notifications, in all their various forms, from email to texts to Facebook posts, can interfere with our peace of mind and our ability to remain immune to interruptions when we just want to be alone for a while. Notifications can also interfere with our focus on work or our personal life. When we turn on push notifications for individual apps and devices, we especially open ourselves to interruptions that take up our time unnecessarily. Some experts advise that, for our peace of mind and ability to focus, we should turn off "notifications" for most of our apps on our smartphones and other devices.[211] But not all push technology is bad. Push technology allows us to get real-time messages from loved ones or real-time news reports based on our interests, which we established on our devices' settings and in our software.

The push concept extends beyond information from companies that have something to sell. Government agencies are putting so much information on websites and social media that we must use this technology to find out what our government is doing and to obtain needed services. For example, I must go online to arrange special trash pickups and to report potholes and other local city problems, although I consider this a convenience, since it saves me a phone call. On the national level, the US Census Bureau is considering encouraging us to complete census survey forms online. These outreach efforts by national, state, and local governments all have the effect of establishing new expectations about our technology use.

We can expect that the use of push technology to expand in the future because that is how advertisers and others get our attention and entice us into spending money. Push technology may be driven by processes that track a lot of information about us so devices can push just the right thing in our direction when they decide to do so. Consider all the online ads that

Smart Tip

Consider turning off some of the notifications on your high-tech devices. Try to find the source of each notification, which may be hidden deep in an app or in the settings of an online store. Then think carefully about whether you really want to stop your life for each notification, or if life would be calmer with fewer of these interruptions. Review the settings for your notifications every six months or so, because new ones can appear out of nowhere.

suddenly appear in front of us that curiously tie to something we may have searched for using Google or on Amazon. Think about all the pestering phone calls to sell us something we are probably not interested in. Advertisers are frequently guided by "big data analytics," in which computers search large databases that zero in on individuals and their preferences.

We need to realize that when we allow push technology in our lives, we may be inadvertently encouraging the invasion of our own privacy and causing the amount of spam we receive to increase over time. We email and text all the time. We sometimes answer our phones when they ring without checking caller ID, letting robot spam callers know there is someone alive and well at our phone number so they can call again and again. By responding quickly to texts, email, and calls, we establish an expectation that we are reachable all the time, leading to further invasion of our privacy with more texts, emails, and calls.

Of course, we may get "jittery" when we aren't connected all the time. Even a trip to a remote beach can be traumatic if there is no internet connectivity. So maybe we really don't want to be left alone. The price of being connected, however, is to alert the world that we can be found and interrupted, so it can push things at us, whether we want them or not. We can anticipate less and less "alone time" in the future if we continue to encourage interruptions by responding quickly to them.

Smart Tip

Consider not responding quickly to incoming emails and calls. Very few of them need to be responded to right away, and they can needlessly interrupt what we are doing.

Key Points

- While it might be hard to imagine, since we already live in a technology-enabled world, there will be much more technology around us in the future.
- We are moving in the direction of self-driving cars, but truly autonomous or driverless cars are still a way off.
- With self-driving cars poised to gain in popularity, there are still challenges that need to be overcome, such as having these cars deal successfully with road construction, snow and ice, low visibility, pedestrians, bicycles, and children playing near the street. The likely date of fully autonomous self-driving cars is 2030.
- Computers that employ artificial intelligence (AI) are beginning to look like they are intelligent. Most of the appearance of a computer being smart is misleading, however, in part because a computer "looks smart," when it is really just doing a lot of very simple things, very fast.
- Several very smart people are concerned that AI could eventually spell doom for humankind because AI will lead to technology being "too smart"! But it is hard to conceive that we can build a machine in the foreseeable future with the kind of generalized AI to make this a reality.

Continued next page

Key Points, continued

- We are becoming surrounded by high-tech assistants that listen to what we say and take actions based on our words, and they will become much smarter over the next several years. Smart speakers and other voice-driven personal assistants will become so good that we will become very dependent on them, rather than treat them as a "curiosity."
- Electronic devices, the heart and soul of new technology, will continue to get faster and more capable, largely using innovative parallel architecture rather than faster electronic components.
- We are constantly faced with "push" technology, notifications on top of notifications and other things that interrupt our work and personal lives. We can turn off some of these notifications and probably enjoy life more!

CHAPTER 11

CONTINUING TO LOVE OUR NEW TECHNOLOGY

AS OUR JOURNEY TOGETHER comes to an end, I hope you have enjoyed reading about new technology, how it all came to be, what it will soon become, and how we can best thrive and survive while using it. It is fair for us to conclude that some of this new technology is too smart, and we shouldn't be forced to adopt all the latest gadgets if we don't want to. We want our technology to be smart, but not too smart. We should take steps to stay in charge of our technology and not let it outsmart us. We don't have to let technology watch us and listen to us and lead us around all the time, although it sometimes feels like we have no choice.

The future looks bright for even more technology in our lives. That's hard to imagine, when it seems that so many things around us listen to us, talk to us, and help us do so much already. But we are still in the infancy of being surrounded by new technology that will be able to partner with us all day long, at home and at work and when we are on the go.

Is there a technological nirvana in our future? No, there's not. But there is a world in which new technological developments will play an increasingly important role in making our lives better. Hopefully, this will be a world in which we will be partners with our technological assistants — and they will do what we want them to do while not intruding too much into our lives.

We have an active role to play in deciding how many high-tech devices we will buy, how many bells and whistles they will have, and how we will use them. We do have to pick and choose from among the alternatives that are available to us, so we are dependent on the developers and marketers of new, high-tech products and services to provide us with great choices, and to provide these choices in a way we can afford them. We may not have a choice about using new technology in some cases. If we want to drive a car, we have to live with the technology that comes with it, although we do have some say about features in this process when we buy or rent a car. Likewise, when we buy a new TV it will most likely contain high-tech features, but we can, however, choose to not use some of that technology to protect our privacy or for other reasons.

You don't have to take a lot of your time to evaluate what technology is doing for you or to you, but it may help you enjoy life more if you spend a little time thinking about it. You want to benefit as much as possible from new technology while also minimizing its possible adverse effects. Enjoy what new technology can do for you and take full advantage of it.

Will we continue to love our technology? Yes, we will! We will love it even more if we are more knowledgeable about that new technology and what it will be able to do for us over the next decade and longer. Thanks for reading my thoughts and observations about new technology. I hope you find the tips included in this book helpful as you choose new high-tech gadgets and as you take a proactive role as a partner with your technology.

ACKNOWLEDGMENTS

I would like to thank my good friend, Hal Shelton, for his continuing inspiration as I started thinking about this book, then writing it, and for reviewing an early draft. Hal beat me to press by over three years with his bestselling book. Special thanks to Marla Markman, who has done a great job as my editor and project manager. I very much appreciate the time that my friends and colleagues, Carl Staton and Bill Lay, and my long-time friend, Perry Klein, have taken to review the manuscript and to provide excellent suggestions. My two wonderful sons, Christopher and Alexander Pyke, have both taken the time to humor their dad as he began this project and to provide helpful suggestions for improving multiple drafts. I thank my wife, Shawn Harris, for her support as I have spent so much time writing and rewriting. I am indebted to all my friends and colleagues over the years. I have learned a lot from everyone I have worked with and collaborated with. In this book, I have touched on a few of the many subjects we explored together over the years.

ABOUT THE AUTHOR

Tom Pyke has over 40 years of experience as an engineering and science leader, and he has spent his career keeping up with and ahead of new technology. He began his career by leading research and standards development in computer networking, systems, and software at the National Bureau of Standards (now known as the National Institute of Standards and Technology).[212] He then led the nation's civil weather satellite program as assistant administrator of the National Oceanic and Atmospheric Administration (NOAA), created NOAA's high-performance computing program, and was NOAA's first chief information officer (CIO). Following NOAA, he became the CIO of the Department of Commerce and then the CIO of the Department of Energy, and he was an executive advisor with Booz Allen Hamilton. He has served on the editorial board of a professional journal, was a member of several professional honorary societies, and has received numerous awards for his accomplishments. He received a BS in electrical engineering from Carnegie Mellon University as a Westinghouse Scholar and an MSE from the University of Pennsylvania as a Ford Foundation Fellow.

ENDNOTES

Introduction

1 Jessica Davis, "Ransomware attack on Connecticut provider impacts 24,000 patients," HealthITSecurity.com, February 5, 2019.

2 Jack Stewart, "Why Tesla's autopilot can't see a stopped firetruck," Wired.com, August 27, 2018.

3 Chenda Ngak, "Baby monitor hacked, spies on Texas child," CBSNews.com, August 13, 2013.

4 Hamza Shaban, "An Amazon Echo recorded a family's conversation, then sent it to a random person in their contacts, report says," WashingtonPost.com, May 25, 2018.

Chapter 1: Surrounded by New Technology

5 "Collision avoidance system," Wikipedia, as of May 20, 2016.

6 Elizabeth Dunn & Michael Norton, *Happy Money*: *The Science of Happier Spending,* reprint ed. (Simon & Schuster, 2014); Heidi Grant Halvorson, "How to keep happiness from fading," August 15, 2002, in *The Science of Success*, reprinted in *Psychology Today*, PsychologyToday.com as of June 3, 2015.

7 Andrew Perrin, "Declining share of Americans would find it very hard to give up TV," PewResearch.org, May 3, 2018.

8 L. D'Acci, "Measuring well-being and progress," *Social Indicators Research*, vol. 104, no. 1, 2010, pp. 47–65.

9 "A world transformed: What are the top 30 innovations of the last 30 years?" Knowledge@Wharton.upenn.edu, February 18, 2009.

10 Nicholas Carr, *The Glass Cage* (Norton, 2014), p. 172; "Technological momentum," Wikipedia, as of June 11, 2015.

11 "Technological determinism," Wikipedia, as of September 18, 2015.

Chapter 2: New Technology Euphoria

12 "Maslow's hierarchy of needs," Wikipedia, as of July 2, 2015.

13 "Maslow's hierarchy," Wikipedia.

14 Michael Hanlon, "The golden quarter," Aeon.co, as of July 2, 2015.
15 Peep Laja, "9 Things to know about influencing purchasing decisions," Conversionxl.com, as of February 26, 2016.
16 "Samsung warns customers to stop using Galaxy Note 7 immediately; more fires reported," LATimes.com, September 10, 2016.
17 "Samsung Galaxy Note 7, Wikipedia, as of March 25, 2017.
18 Dennis J. Wilkins, "The bathtub curve and product failure behavior: Part one — The bathtub curve, infant mortality and burn-in. Weibull.com, *Reliability Hot Wire*, issue 21, November 2002.
19 Brian Kennedy, "28 percent of Americans are 'strong' early adopters of technology," PewResearch.org, July 12, 2016.

Chapter 3: Downsides of New Technology

20 Andrea Peterson, "How the internet is ruining your memory," *Washington Post*, July 1, 2015.
21 Caitlin Dewey, "Google is making you more forgetful. Here's why that's a good thing," *Washington Post*, October 8, 2015.
22 HIPAA (Health Insurance Portability and Accountability Act of 1996) is U.S. legislation that provides data privacy and security provisions for safeguarding medical information.
23 Carr, *Glass Cage*, p. 207.
24 Maryanne Wolf, "Our 'deep reading' brain: Its digital evolution poses questions," NiemanReports.org, June 29, 2010.
25 Michael G. Williams, "From paper to pixels: The troubling impact of digital reading," *Erickson Tribune*, April 23, 2015.
26 Nathan Hurst, "iPhone separation linked to physiological anxiety, poor cognitive performance, MU study finds," News bureau, University of Missouri, MuNews.Missouri.edu, January 9, 2015; and Elizabeth Armstrong, "iPhone separation anxiety is real, study says," Newser, January 12, 2015.
27 Hurst, "iPhone separation."
28 Luisa Dillner, "Does 'phone separation anxiety' really exist?" TheGuardian.com, August 28, 2017.
29 Nicola Davies, "Nomophobia: The modern-day pathology," PsychiatryAdvisor.com, September 18, 2018.
30 Nick Bilton, "The health concerns in wearable tech," NYTimes.com, March 18, 2015.
31 "Screens before bedtime harm sleep. The effect is biggest for teenagers," *The Economist*, May 10, 2015.
32 "Technological unemployment," Wikipedia, as of March 29, 2017.
33 "Automation and anxiety," Special report, *The Economist*, June 25, 2016.
34 Federica Cocco, "Most U.S. manufacturing jobs lost to technology, not trade," *Financial Times*, December 2, 2016.
35 "How productive is the U.S.?" *Bloomberg Businessweek*, March 2–March 8, 2015, p. 16.

36 Robert J. Samuelson, "Robots in the workplace," *Washington Post*, March 15, 2015.

37 David Rotman, "How technology is destroying jobs," *MIT Technology Review*, June 12, 2013.

38 David L. Strayer, Frank A. Drews, & Dennis J. Crouch, "Fatal distraction? A comparison of the cell-phone driver and the drunk driver," Department of Psychology, University of Utah.

39 "How to save phone-using motorists from themselves," *The Economist*, April 25, 2015.

40 "Understanding the distracted brain," National Safety Council white paper, April 2012.

41 Frederick Kuinkle, "More evidence that smartphones and driving don't mix," WashingtonPost.com, April 4, 2017.

42 "Risks to hands-free driving," Editorial board, *New York Times*, May 28, 2015.

43 "In study, texting lifts crash risk by large margin," *New York Times*, July 27, 2009; "April is distracted driving awareness month," Virginia Tech Transportation Institute, http://www.vtti.vt.edu, as of May 20, 2015.

44 Tony Romm, "ICE is tapping into a huge license-plate database, ACLU says, raising new privacy concerns about surveillance," WashingtonPost.com, March 13, 2019.

45 "After Boston: The pros and cons of surveillance cameras," CNN.com, April 26, 2013.

46 Josh Sanburn, "Shots fired," *Time*, October 2, 2017.

47 David Kravets, "An intentional mistake: The anatomy of Google's wi-fi sniffing debacle," Wired.com, May 2, 2012.

48 Declan McCullagh & Anne Broache, "CNET news — Cell phone eavesdropping technique 'functioned whether the phone was powered on or off,'" PrivacyCase.com, December 1, 2006.

49 Darlene Storm, "Remotely listen in via hacked VoIP phones: Cisco working on eavesdropping patch," *Computerworld*, September 13, 2015; "Cyber defense magazine — Smartphones in the business environment: Trusted tool or trusted threat?," http://www.privacycase.com, as of September 15, 2015; "Cellphone surveillance," Wikipedia, as of September 15, 2015.

50 Tim Stenovec, "Google has gotten incredibly good at predicting traffic — and here's how," BusinessInsider.com, December 18, 2015; Ryan Nakashima, "AP Exclusive: Google tracks your movements, like it or not," APNews.com, August 13, 2018.

51 Kim Komando, "Your car's hidden 'black box' and how to keep it private," USAToday.com, December 26, 2014.

52 Jeff Plungis, "You're never alone in your car," *Consumer Reports*, June 2018.

53 Andrea Peterson & Hayley Tsukayama, "How Apple is trying to protect your privacy as its products get more personal," *Washington Post*, September 29, 2015.

54 Puneet Sikka, "How Facebook and other social networks monetize users' data," MarketRealist.com, September 26, 2014; Janko Roettgers, "Facebook admits to scanning private messages, releases privacy policy updates," Variety.com, April 4, 2018; Craig Timberg, Tony Romm, & Elizabeth Dwoskin, "Facebook said 'malicious actors' used its tools to discover identities and collect data on a massive global scale," WashingtonPost.com, April 4, 2018.

55 Farhad Manjoo, "iPhone 6s's hands-free Siri is an omen of the future," *New York Times*, September 22, 2015.

56 "Get started with Windows 10," Windows.Microsoft.com, as of September 22, 2015.

57 "Alexa and Alexa device FAQs," Amazon.com, as of May 11, 2016.

58 Sarah E. Needleman & Parmy Olson, "Google contractors listen to recordings of people using virtual assistant," *Wall Street Journal*, July 11, 2019.

59 "What your smart TV knows about you," *Consumer Reports*, May 2018.

60 Hayley Tsukayama, "These smart TVs were apparently spying on their owners," WashingtonPost.com, February 6, 2017.

61 "Miss Teen USA: Screamed upon learning she was 'sextortion' victim," CNN.com, September 28, 2013.

62 James K. Wilcox, "How to turn off smart TV snooping features," *Consumer Reports*. The article can be found at https://www.consumerreports.org/privacy/how-to-turn-off-smart-tv-snooping-features.

63 "Report: Some top baby monitors vulnerable to hackers," CBSNews.com, September 2, 2015.

64 Samuel Gibbs, "Privacy fears over 'smart' Barbie that can listen to your kids," TheGuardian.com, March 13, 2015.

65 "Data privacy and smart meters," a publication of the SmartGrid consumer collaborative, distributed by Dominion Virginia Power through http://www.dominionenergy.com.

66 Manjoo, "iPhone 6's hands-free Siri"; David Pierce, "We're on the brink of a revolution in crazy-smart digital assistants," Wired.com, September 16, 2015.

67 Christina Medici Scolaro, "Why Google's Eric Schmidt says the 'internet will disappear'," CNBC.com, January 23, 2015.

68 "Mobile giants: "Please don't share the where," KrebsonSecurity.com, May 22, 2018.

69 Robert X. Cringley, "The new Bill Gates: A revisionist look at the richest man on earth," PBS.org, November 23, 2000.

70 M. Weiser, R. Gold, & J. S. Brown, "The origins of ubiquitous computing research at PARC in the late 1980s," *IBM Systems Journal*, 38, no. 4, 1999.

71 David Sax, "Why physical things matter in a digital world," *Time*, November 14, 2016.

Chapter 4: Watch Out for Cybersecurity

72 "Federal cybersecurity risk determination report and action plan," Office of Management and Budget, May 2018.

73 Taylor Armerding, "The OPM breach report: A long time coming," CSOonline.com, October 13, 2016.

74 The Google Play store is at Play.Google.com.

75 "App store review guidelines," Developer.Apple.com, as of April 4, 2017.

76 Sarah Perez, "App submissions of Google Play now reviewed by staff, will include age-based ratings," TechCrunch.com, March 17, 2015.

77 Marc Goodman, *Future Crimes: Everything Is Connected, Everyone Is Vulnerable, and What We Can Do about It* (Doubleday, 2015).

78 Lorrie Cranor, "Time to rethink mandatory password changes," Federal Trade Commission, FTC.gov, March 2, 2016.

79 The term "jailbroken" means that a smartphone or smart tablet has had its operating system software modified to reduce restrictions on the device, allowing users, for example, to download any app or to reset defaults for web browsers and other functions. Users can change the look and feel of a jailbroken device based on personal preferences. But jailbreaking can reduce protection from cyberattacks and other threats that are built in to the original device software.

80 Selena Larson, "Please stop charging your phone in public ports," Money.CNN.com, February 16, 2017.

81 "Credit freeze FAQs," Federal Trade Commission, Consumer.FTC.gov, as of June 18, 2019.

82 Kate Silver, "Avoid ATMs on weekends, choose your gas pump wisely and other tips to keep your finances safe when traveling," WashingtonPost.com, April 3, 2018.

83 Nick Watt, Claire Pedersen, & John Kapetaneas, "Why you're still not safe from fraud if you have a credit card with a chip," ABC-News.go.com, April 12, 2016.

Chapter 5: Technology—A Historical Perspective

84 Alan Boyle, "Oldest stone tools go back 3.3 million years, predating our species," NBCNews.com, May 20, 2015; "The oldest tool in the world," *The Economist*, May 23, 2015.

85 "Timeline of historic inventions," Wikipedia, as of February 25, 2015.

86 "The Babbage engine," ComputerHistory.org, as of May 21, 2015.

87 "Inventions 1900 to 1990," HistoryLearningSite.co.uk, as of February 25, 2015.

88 "This day in history, September 9, 1947: First instance of actual computer bug being found," ComputerHistory.org, as of February 21, 2017.
89 Boris Veldhulijzen Van Zanten, "The very first recorded computer bug," TheNextWeb.com, September 18, 2013.
90 Walter Isaacson, *The Innovators* (Simon and Schuster, 2014), p. 81.
91 Isaacson, *Innovators*, p. 81.
92 "A brief history of British computers: The first 25 years (1948-1973)," BCS.org, as of June 13, 2015.
93 "SEAC (computer)," Wikipedia, as of June 13, 2015.
94 "UNIVAC I," Wikipedia, as of June 13, 2015.
95 Thomas N. Pyke, Jr., "Time-shared computer systems," *Advances in Computers, Vol. 8* (Academic Press, 1967), pp. 1–45.
96 Pyke, "Time-shared computer systems."
97 "MITS Altair 8800 computer," OldComputers.net, as of August 21, 2019.
98 "Apple I," Applemuseum.bott.org, as of August 21, 2019.
99 Michael A. Hiltzik, *Dealers of Lightning* (Harper Business, 1999); Douglas K. Smith & Robert C. Alexander, *Fumbling the Future* (William Morrow, 1988).
100 "Ethernet," Wikipedia, as of February 23, 2018.
101 "Metcalfe's law," Wikipedia, as of May 24, 2019.
102 "AOL," Wikipedia, as of September 17, 2015.
103 ARPA, the Advanced Research Projects Agency, is an agency of the US Department of Defense. It is now known as DARPA, the Defense Advanced Projects Agency.
104 The ARPANET initially consisted of interface message processors (IMPs) connected to each other through telephone lines. The IMPs were each connected to one or more computers. IMPs provided reliable communication of messages divided into packets and routed them to destination IMPs, sometimes sending packets by alternate paths through the network and then assembling the entire message at the destination end. Terminal interface message processors were IMPs with a capability added to allow teletypewriter and display terminals to connect to the ARPANET without going through an attached computer.
105 "Internet Timeline," Infoplease.com, as of June 14, 2015.
106 From 1994 to 2001, the author led one of the first transaction-based applications using the web. This was the GLOBE (Global Learning and Observations to Benefit the Environment) Program, an Internet-based environmental science and education program for students. In GLOBE, students make environmental measurements near their schools and enter the resulting data through the Internet into servers so it can be shared with other student scientists and with professional scientists. Students around the world then observe images of the world built using these student data from throughout

the world and learn about science and about each other. Over 20 years later, the GLOBE Program is still going strong, with participation by students in more than 35,000 schools in 121 countries.

107 "Netscape," Wikipedia, as of September 17, 2015.

108 J. C. R. Licklider, "Man-computer symbiosis," *IRE Transactions on Human Factors in Electronics*, vol. HFE-1, no. 1, March 1960, pp. 4–11.

109 "Hypertext," Wikipedia, as of June 16, 2015.

110 "Andries van Dam," Wikipedia, as of June 16, 2015.

111 CERN stands for *Conseil Européen pour la Recherche Nucléaire.* Isaacson, *Innovators,* p. 412.

112 Isaacson, *Innovators,* p. 416.

113 Isaacson, *Innovators,* p. 418.

114 Isaacson, *Innovators,* p. 418.

115 Jefferson Graham, "New streaming TV boxes for fall," *USA Today*, October 9, 2015.

116 "Works with NEST," Nest.com, as of March 9, 2017.

Chapter 6: Everything Is So Complex

117 Denning & Denning, "Cybersecurity is harder."

118 Bob O'Donnell, "Your average car is a lot more code-driven than you think," USAToday.com, June 28, 2016.

119 "Vastly faster and energy-efficient wireless," *Kiplinger Letter Tech Alerts*, April 29, 2015; "FCC notice of inquiry on the matter of use of spectrum bands above 24GHz for mobile radio services," Federal Communications Commission, RM-11664, October 17, 2014.

120 Thomas N. Pyke, Jr., "Anticipation for remote computing," *Proceedings ACM National Conference*, 1978.

121 Richard Vonck, "Connecting with our connected world," *The Futurist*, November–December 2013.

122 Clicking on a link to a Web page results in a lookup on a "domain name server" to get the numerical Internet Protocol (IP) address (which is the identifier for a server computer on the internet) that corresponds to the web link. This numerical IP address is then sent through internet routers to the corresponding server computer to locate the web page. The web page is then sent from that server computer back to our smartphone or PC through internet routers, using its IP address.

123 David Gelles, Hiroko Tabuchi, & Matthew Dolan, "The weak spot under the hood," *New York Times*, September 27, 2015.

124 Gelles, Tabuchi, & Dolan, "Weak spot."

125 Fergal Toomeyu, "Why latency management will decide the future of the IoT," http://www.corvil.com/blog/2015/why-latency-management-future-internet-of-things, April 15, 2015.

126 Chris Talbot, "Cisco intercloud aims for workload portability in hybrid clouds," ChannelFutures.com, January 30, 2014.

127 "Three minutes: Internet pioneer looks ahead," ABCNews.go.com, November 3, 2005.

128 Sara Robinson, "Cut in fiber cable disrupts internet traffic nationwide," NYTimes.com, September 30, 1999.

129 The internet domain name system is a hierarchical set of server computers on the internet that translate human readable host computer names into IP (numerical) addresses that are used in communication between internet host computers and with any device connected to the internet that has an IP address, such as a PC, a smartphone, or an Internet of Things device.

130 Nicky Woolf, "DDoS attack that disrupted internet was largest of its kind in history, experts say," TheGuardian.com, October 26, 2016.

131 Brian Krebs," Hacked cameras, DVRs powered today's massive internet outage," KrebsonSecurity.com, October 16, 2016.

132 Carr, *Glass Cage,* p. 156.

133 Don Norman, *The Design of Everyday Things*: *Revised and Expanded Edition* (Basic Books, 2013).

134 "J. D. Power and Associates," Wikipedia, as of May 30, 2017.

Chapter 8: The Things Are Coming!

135 "Gartner identifies top 10 strategic IoT technologies and trends," Gartner.com, November 7, 2018.

136 George Parrett, "Consumers slow to connect with IoT in the home," Deloitte LLP, a UK market view, Deloitte.com, July 19, 2016.

137 Mark Weiser, "The computer for the 21st century," *Scientific American*, vol. 265, no. 3, 1991, pp. 66–75.

138 "Cyber-physical systems homepage," NIST.gov, as of September 2, 2015.

139 The attack surface is the total number of different points through which a cybersecurity attacker can attempt to penetrate a system.

140 Steve Weisman, "Are you safe in the Internet of Things?," *USA Today*, April 4, 2015.

141 James Stavridis & Dave Weinstein, "The Internet of Things is a cyberwar nightmare," ForeignPolicy.com, November 3, 2016; Krebs, "Hacked cameras."

142 Weisman, "Are you safe?"

143 "Securing the Internet of Things," Security tip (ST17-001), US-cert.gov, November 16, 2017.

144 "Internet of Things: Privacy and security in a connected world," Federal Trade Commission staff report, January 2015.

145 Erica Fink & Laurie Segall, "Your TV might be watching you," CNN Money, August 1, 2013.

146 "Baby monitor hacker delivers creepy message to child," CBSNews.com, April 23, 2015; "Hacker 'shouts abuse' via Foscam baby monitoring camera," BBC News, August 14, 2013.

147 Amy B Wang, "'I'm in your baby's room': A hacker took over a baby monitor and broadcast threats, parents say," WashingtonPost.com, December 20, 2018.

Chapter 9: How to Survive New Technology

148 Laura Roman, "Information overload? Not everybody is feeling it, Pew study says," NPR.org, December 7, 2016.
149 "Moderation," Wikipedia, as of July 6, 2017; "The wisdom of the Greeks: Moderation in all things," PsychologyToday.com, December 17, 2010.
150 "Steve Jobs Quotable Quote," Goodreads.com, as of March 10, 2017.

Chapter 10: What's in Our Future?

151 Tim Higgins, "Google's self-driving car program odometer reaches 2 million miles," *Wall Street Journal*, October 6, 2016.
152 "Cars with Autopilot in 2019," AutoPilotReview.com, as of June 1, 2019.
153 Jordan Golson, "Tesla updates Autopilot, Autosteer now works to 80 mph in new cars," TheVerge.com, March 29, 2017.
154 Jack Stewart, "Tesla's new 'Autopilot' is just the start of a critical reboot," Wired.com, January 24, 2017.
155 Higgins, "Google's self-driving car program."
156 Graham Rapier, "Waymo One passengers reveal what it's really like to ride in Alphabet's self-driving taxis," BusinessInsider.com, February 6, 2019; Andrew J. Haskins, "We spoke to a Waymo One customer about how robot taxis get confused by rainstorms," TheVerge.com, January 20, 2019.
157 Tom Randall, "Tesla's Autopilot vindicated with 40 percent drop in crashes," Bloomberg.com, January 19, 2017.
158 Adrienne Lafrance, "Self-driving cars could save 300,000 lives per decade in America," TheAtlantic.com, September 29, 2015.
159 Aarian Marshall, "Why self-driving cars *can't even* with construction zones," Wired.com, February 10, 2017; Peter Holley, "How do you get people to trust autonomous vehicles? This company is giving them 'virtual eyes,'" WashingtonPost.com, August 29, 2018.
160 Mike Spector, Jack Nicas, & Mike Ramsey, "Tesla's Autopilot vexes some drivers, even its fans," WSJ.com, July 6, 2016.
161 Jacob Bogage, "Tesla driver using Autopilot killed in crash," *Washington Post*, June 30, 2016.
162 Drew Harwell, "Carmakers' automated dilemma: How to keep drivers from feeling robotic," *Washington Post*, May 24, 2015.
163 "Autonomous vehicle awareness rising, acceptance declining, according to Cox automotive study," Press.Autotrader.com, August 16, 2018.
164 Alistair Barr & Mike Ramsey, "Google tries to make its cars drive more like humans," *Wall Street Journal*, September 28, 2015.

165 Barr & Ramsey, "Google tries."
166 Alex Davies, "The case for making self-driving cars think like humans," Wired.com, February 5, 2016.
167 "Pittsburgh left," Wikipedia.com, as of April 8, 2018.
168 Jeffrey Mervis, "Are we going too fast on driverless cars?" *Science Magazine*, December 14, 2017.
169 Matt McFarland, "Tesla's promise of 'full-self-driving' angers autonomous vehicle experts," CNN.com, March 2, 2019; Eric Evarts, "Tesla Autopilot ranks next-to-last in study of self-driving systems," GreenCarReports.com, March 22, 2019.
170 Jim Collins, "The auto industry is nowhere near the on-ramp for self-driving cars," Forbes.com, June 17, 2019.
171 John Koetsier, "Self-driving Cars in 10 Years: EU expects 'fully automated' cars by 2030," Forbes.com, April 6, 2019.
172 "The singularity is near," Wikipedia, as of May 27, 2015; Ray Kurzweil, *The Age of Spiritual Machines* (Viking, 1999), p. 278.
173 "Technological singularity," Wikipedia, as of June 1, 2015.
174 "Intelligence," Wikipedia, as of September 28, 2015; "Intelligence," TheFreeDictionary.com, as of September 28, 2015.
175 Vivek Wadhwa, "The coming problem of our iPhones being more intelligent than us," Washingtonpost.com, April 23, 2015.
176 Katherine Bourzac, "A deep learning AI chip for your phone," *IEEE Spectrum*, February 4, 2016.
177 Will Knight, "IBM pushes deep learning with a Watson upgrade," TechnologyReview.com, July 9, 2015.
178 "IBM and NVIDIA team up on world's fastest deep learning enterprise solution," IBM.com, November 14, 2016.
179 Michael Irving, "For its next trick, IBM's Watson tackles your taxes," NewAtlas.com, February 1, 2017.
180 "Google, Microsoft take voice-search to new levels," *USA Today*, March 30, 2015.
181 Katherine Bourzac, "To get AI in everyday gadgets, engineers go to specialized hardware," Spectrum.IEEE.org, February 14, 2017.
182 Elon Musk, speaking at the MIT Aeronautics and Astronautics department's Centennial Symposium in October 2014, as quoted in the article by Peter Holley, "Bill Gates on the dangers of artificial intelligence: 'I don't understand why some people are not concerned,'" *Washington Post*, January 29, 2015.
183 Eliene Augenbraun, "Elon Musk: Artificial intelligence may be 'more dangerous than nukes,'" CBS News, August 4, 2014.
184 Peter Holley, "Stephen Hawking just got an artificial intelligence upgrade, but still thinks AI could bring an end of mankind," *Washington Post*, December 2, 2014.
185 T. J. Deitsch, "Stephen Hawking predicts robot apocalypse coming within 100 years," Geek.com, May 13, 2015.

186 "Apple co-founder Steve Wozniak on the Apple Watch, electric cars and the surpassing of humanity," *Australian Financial Review Magazine*, March 24, 2015.

187 Holley, "Bill Gates on dangers."

188 Carr, *Glass Cage,* p. 207.

189 Licklider, "Man-Computer Symbiosis," pp. 4–11. See Chapter 1 for a summary of how Licklider's work built on concepts stated by Vannevar Bush in his famous 1945 *Atlantic Monthly* article, "As We May Think."

190 Pyke, "Time-shared computer systems."

191 "NLS (Computer system)," Wikipedia, as of March 11, 2017.

192 John E. Kelly, III, & Steve Hamm, *Smart Machines* (Columbia University Press, 2013), p. 7.

193 Garry Kasparov, "The chess master and the computer," *New York Review of Books*, February 11, 2010.

194 Isaacson, *Innovators,* p. 478.

195 "New study suggests guidelines for takeover time in automated vehicles," Phys.org, January 26, 2017.

196 David Mindell, *Our Robots, Ourselves*: *Robotics and the myths of autonomy* (Viking/Penguin, 2015); Jeremy Hsu, "Q&A: Why fully autonomous robot cars hail from the 20th century," *IEEE Spectrum*, October 23, 2015.

197 Ethan Sacks, "Alexa privacy fail highlights risks of smart speakers," NBCNews.com, May 26, 2018.

198 Laura Stevens & Tripp Mickle, "Alexa and Siri escalate battle of virtual assistants," *Wall Street Journal*, September 1, 2017.

199 "Google Home starts to catch up," Consumer Intelligence Research Partners, LLC, February 12, 2018; Nat Levy, "Amazon passes 10M Alexa-powered devices sold, survey says, with more models on the way," Geekwire.com, May 8, 2017.

200 Jeff Dunn, "We put Siri, Alexa, Google Assistant, and Cortana through a marathon of tests to see who's winning the virtual assistant race — Here's what we found," Businessinsider.com, November 4, 2016; "Cortana is your truly personal digital assistant," Microsoft.com, as of September 13, 2017.

201 Geoffrey A. Fowler, "Hey, Alexa, come clean about how much you're really recording us," Washingtonpost.com, May 24, 2018.

202 Matthew Kassel, "Alexa, Just how secure are you?," *Wall Street Journal*, May 30, 2018.

203 Gordon E. Moore states that the complexity for minimum component costs has increased at a rate of roughly a factor of two per year. "Certainly over the short term this rate can be expected to continue, if not to increase. Over the longer term, this rate of increase is a bit more uncertain, although there is no reason to believe it will not remain nearly constant for at least 10 years," "Cramming more components onto integrated circuits," *Electronics*

Magazine, April 19, 1965, p. 4; Gordon E. Moore, "Cramming more components onto integrated circuits," *Proceedings IEEE*, vol. 86, no. 1, January 1998.

204 "Moore's Law," Wikipedia, as of April 3, 2015.

205 "Transistor count," Wikipedia, as of April 17, 2015.

206 See Chapter 3, where the author describes bringing technology with this capability to Washington, DC, in 1977.

207 Andrew Huang, "The death of Moore's law will spur innovation," IEEE Spectrum online, posted March 31, 2015.

208 Peter Mortensen, "Why multi core processors?," Superuser.com, August 21, 2010.

209 "Apple A11," Wikipedia, as of March 24, 2018.

210 Adrian Kingsley-Hughes, "Inside Apple's new A11 bionic processor," Zdnet.com, September 12, 2017.

211 David Pierce, "Turn off your push notifications. All of them," Wired.com, July 23, 2017.

About the Author

212 His team set up and used a research node of the ARPANET, which, together with the NSFNET, evolved into the internet. He was a partner with computer science researchers worldwide, and he led the creation of early US government cybersecurity guidance. He brought innovative Xerox PARC (Palo Alto Research Center) technology to Washington, to the White House, House, and Senate, and to NBS, two years before Steve Jobs saw it and developed the Apple Mac.

ENDNOTES IN THE SMART TIPS, KEY WORDS, AND SHADED BOXES

Chapter 1

213 Robb Rutledge, "A computational and neural model of happiness," RobbRutledge.com, August 8, 2014.

Chapter 2

214 "Bleeding edge technology," Wikipedia, as of March 19, 2016.

215 Peter J. Denning & Dorothy E. Denning, "Cybersecurity is harder than building bridges," *American Scientist*, vol. 104, May–June 2016.

Chapter 3

216 "2015 Edelman Trust Barometer executive summary," released at 2015 World Economic Forum, summarized in *Time*, February 9, 2015.

Chapter 4

217 "Extended fraud alerts and credit freezes," Federal Trade Commission, Consumer.FTC.gov, as of March 11, 2019.

218 US Department of Homeland Security, "Parents and educators tip card"; "Stop. Think. Connect. National cybersecurity awareness campaign. Kids presentation," DHS.gov, as of May 1, 2016.

Chapter 5

219 "Technology," Wikipedia, as of June 19, 2015.
220 "First technologies: Fire and tools," UShistory.org, as of August 21, 2019.

Chapter 6

221 "Facts & figures," Akamai.com, as of May 27, 2019.

Chapter 7

222 "David Bradley (engineer)," Wikipedia, as of October 5, 2018.
223 Tom Warren, "Bill Gates admits control-alt-delete was a mistake, blames IBM," TheVerge.com, September 26, 2013.

Chapter 8

224 "Fog computing and the Internet of Things: Extend the cloud to where the things are," Cisco white paper, April 2015, available from https://www.cisco.com/c/dam/en_us/solutions/trends/iot/docs/computing-overview.pdf; Michaela Iorga, Larry Feldman, Robert Barton, Michael J. Martin, Nedim Goren, & Charif Mahmoudi,"Fog computing conceptual model," NIST special publication 500-325, NIST.gov, March 2018.

Chapter 9

225 Schumpeter, "Too much information," Economist.com, June 30, 2011.
226 David Weinberger, "The problem with the data-information-knowledge-wisdom hierarchy," *Harvard Business Review*, February 2, 2010.
227 J. Peder Zane, "In the age of information, specializing to survive," *New York Times*, March 19, 2015.
228 Alvin Toffler, *Future Shock* (Random House, 1970).
229 "Exabyte," Wikipedia, as of March 29, 2015.
230 Andrew Cave, "What will we do when the world's data hits 163 zettabytes in 2025?," Forbes.com, April 13, 2017.
231 Ian Burrell, "The Times' newsroom set to ring with the sounds of typewriters once more," Independent.co.uk, August 26, 2014.
232 "Russian guard service reverts to typewriters after NSA leaks," *The Guardian*, July 11, 2013.

Chapter 10

233 "Artificial neural network," Wikipedia, as of July 13, 2015.
234 Alfred Ng, "Amazon Alexa transcripts live on, even after you delete voice records," Cnet.com, May 9, 2019.

INDEX

A

E

F

G

H

I

V

W

Z

Made in the USA
Monee, IL
05 November 2026

67391549R00155